# Sing Anything

## Mastering Vocal Styles

by Gina Latimerlo & Lisa Popeil

Illustrations by Gianni Merlo

# TABLE OF CONTENTS

# INTRODUCTION

While many singers focus years of effort on performing one style of music, our changing world encourages performers to sing in many different styles. <u>Sing Anything</u> is the first book written for singers who are ready to expand their vocal horizons and learn the intricacies of the most widely performed American styles – as well as the basic techniques that underlie them all.

This book contains our combined knowledge of over 65 years of voice study, performance, and teaching in styles such as opera, operetta, musical theater belting, musical theater legit, pop, jazz, R&B, country, and rock. We're excited to share the best tips from our vast experience with you!

Our intention is to get you going in the right direction by providing you with concise instruction in a systematic form. It is important to recognize, however, that training your ears and your muscle memory will take time, dedication, and perseverance. Be sure to be both persistent and patient with yourself as you learn – whether you choose to study by yourself, with a friend, or in lessons with a competent voice teacher.

In addition to vocal technique and style tips, we've also included information covering other interpretive considerations – such as phrasing, 'Stylisms' (like yodeling, growls, and runs) – as well as suggestions on how to achieve emotional expressivity. We also touch on the cultural history of each style. Finally, we'll list our favorite singers so that you can steal from the greats themselves!

Audio tracks are available with this book to help further your learning. These tracks contain both the Stylisms, as well as specific Vocal Exercises for each style. These audio tracks can be downloaded from <u>singanything.com</u>. On the bottom of the homepage, you'll find a login area. Simply input the following information to gain access to the entire site:

> username:    singer
> password:    singnow

You may notice that the Vocal Exercises feature large vocal ranges to accommodate different voice types. Only sing as high or as low as feels comfortable. In a short time, you'll be able to sing with more comfort, skill, and range than ever before. To help you do the Vocal Exercises correctly, be sure to listen carefully to the demonstration vocal. At singanything.com, you'll also find detailed instructions on how to practice the exercises correctly...as well as bonus material such as a Q&A section, sheet music links, and more.

Achieving your highest level of artistic expression requires a strong foundation. That's why we begin with vocal anatomy and the basics of posture, support, and breathing. We hope you enjoy the journey.

# CHAPTER 1
# BODY PARTS AND MUSICAL TERMS

## BODY PARTS

Singing is an athletic event. Done well, you'll be coordinating a number of muscle groups into perfectly aligned and simultaneous activity.

Here is a diagram of some of the anatomy involved in singing:

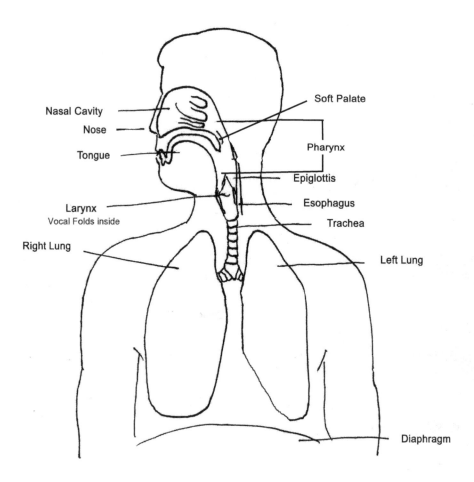

Next, you'll find explanations of what's included in the diagram, as well as other important body parts involved in vocal production.

**Abdominal Muscles:**  Four pairs of muscles located between the ribs and the pelvis (including the waist area).

**Diaphragm:**  The dome-shaped muscle below your lungs that controls breathing.  When it's relaxed, the diaphragm is a high dome; when the diaphragm contracts, it descends and flattens.

**Epigastrium:**  The area directly below the sternum which protrudes when the diaphragm contracts and flattens.

**Epiglottis:**  The 'toilet seat of the voice' – a flap connected to the top of your larynx that closes to protect your windpipe when swallowing food.

**Esophagus:**  The 'food tube' that connects the pharynx to the stomach.

**Hard Palate:**  The hard part of the roof of your mouth.

**Jaw:**  The large bone/muscle combination that attaches to the skull.

**Larynx:**  Your voice box.  Your 'Adam's apple' is the front part of it.  It moves up and down when you swallow.  Your vocal folds sit inside the larynx.

**Lungs:**  The two spongy sacs in your chest used for breathing.

**Nasal Cavity:**  The large space in your head above and behind your nose.

**Nose:**  The facial protuberance that contains the nostrils.  Used for breathing, smelling, and resonating.

**Pharynx:**  The space in your throat above your larynx and behind your mouth and nose.  An important resonating chamber.

**Ribs:**  Semi-circular bones around your chest which protect your lungs and heart.  They aid in breathing.

**Soft Palate:**  The soft, squishy part of the roof of your mouth behind your hard palate (also known as the 'velum').  The soft palate lifts up at the beginning of a yawn and is the main controller of nasality.

**Sternum:**  The bottom-center part of the ribcage where most of your ribs meet.  Below your heart, it's the last hard, boney part you feel before you get to the softer upper belly.

**Tongue:**  The organ inside the mouth which can lengthen, shorten, bend, and twist.  Used for eating.  Used also in speech and singing to shape  resonance and help create different vowel and consonant sounds.

**Trachea:**  The windpipe.  A large tube which connects the pharynx to the bronchial tubes (which then lead to the lungs).

**Vocal Folds:**  (*Vocal Cords*) Two bands of muscle covered in a wet, spongy coating. They vibrate together to create sound.  Located in the larynx.

## MUSICAL TERMS

Here are more definitions for terms you will encounter in the book.

By <u>vocal technique</u>, we mean the physical activities that your body engages in to sing. <u>Tone</u> is the quality (or shade) of the sound – for example, dark and heavy versus light and airy. <u>Resonance</u> is the filtering of the buzzy sound generated by the vibrating vocal folds. It alters the tone and loudness of the voice. <u>Resonance chambers</u> are the spaces between the vocal folds and the end of the lips and nose. <u>Musical interpretation</u> means the choices that a singer makes in order to express a song's emotional content or mood. The term <u>dynamics</u> refers to how loudly or softly one sings. <u>Tempo</u> means the speed of the beat – in other words, how fast or slow the song is played or sung. <u>Rhythm</u> is how long or short notes are held, as well as when they occur. <u>Notes</u> are the actual musical pitches that are sung (*do, re, mi*, etc). <u>Stylisms</u> are vocal effects such as cries, fries, growls, slides, and runs. <u>Vibrato</u> is a regular, cyclical change of pitch. It's an ornament that sounds wavy and expressive (see Stylism #2).

Just to clarify, vocal styles are different than musical styles. In this book, we're focusing on which category the *singer* can be placed in – not necessarily what the *musical accompaniment* sounds like. So, for example, you could conceivably sing a pop-sounding song in an R&B vocal style.

Be sure to check out the Definitions section at the end of the book for more musical terms.

# CHAPTER 2
# YOUR SUPPORT SYSTEM

Now, let's start on the journey of the three C's: Control, Confidence, and Consistency. Without Control of your body, you'll never feel totally Confident in your ability to sing, no matter how naturally talented you might be. And, skilled singers are Consistent singers – they always sound good! To achieve the three C's, you'll need to master the skills of Posture, Support, and Breathing. These skills are the foundation of any sound you want to make, no matter which style of music you choose to sing. Practice these skills carefully and often, and you will be rewarded with the Control you crave, the Confidence you want, and the Consistency you'll need.

## POSTURE

Strong, straight-up posture is a vocal technique common to all styles of singing. Your back will be tall and straight, your chest will be lifted high (like it is hoisted on a hook), and your ribs will be expanded all the way around. Your body-weight will be evenly distributed on feet placed hip-width apart. Your head should be held comfortably high with the back of your neck feeling very long – as 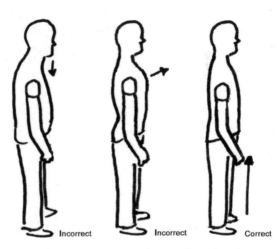 though an imaginary string is pulling you up from the crown of your head. This head position remains constant throughout the entire range of your voice (whether the notes are high or low).

## *Exercise for Posture*
*Stand slightly sideways in front of a mirror and use the following checklist:*

- *feet slightly apart*
- *knees flexed (not locked and not super-bent)*
- *sternum held high*
- *back and side ribs slightly expanded*
- *shoulders relaxed and directly above your hips*
- *back of neck long, but not stiff*
- *weight evenly distributed on both feet*
- *bellies soft while breathing*

# BREATHING

Though there are many ways a body can breathe, the following way is ideal for singers. This method is quiet, invisible, and feels great! It also eliminates that noisy chest breathing that is so common among untrained singers.

Imagine that you're going to breathe into your belly. You should feel your belly RELAXING OUT for breathing. This action pulls the air in using the body's natural 'vacuum effect.'

Although your belly is active, your chest always stays comfortably high and still for the whole breathing process.

When you blow air out – with or without making a sound – your bottom belly will move IN toward your spine.

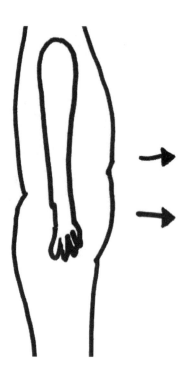

## *Exercise for Breathing*

*Standing tall with good singing posture, place your thumb on your navel and place the remainder of that same hand below. Now exhale on a 'hoo' sound – like trying to blow out candles on a cake – and be sure to keep your chest up. Notice that your lower belly goes in. (Uh oh! Did your chest drop? If so, try again and be sure to keep it up.)*

*Once you have exhaled, it's time to get air back into your body. To breathe in, simply open your mouth, then open your vocal folds (think a wide throat), then slooowly release your bottom belly out. Feel the air come into your body all by itself. Imagine filling your belly with air until you feel satisfied – like you're filling a glass with water from the bottom to the top.*

*Now once again exhale on 'hoo,' feeling your bottom belly pull in. Then, for silent air intake, release lower belly and fill. That's breathing for singers!*

## SUPPORT

One essential skill to master for a lifetime of great singing is 'support.' Short for 'abdominal breath support,' support is really the engine of the voice – it makes the voice go. It refers to the actions of the muscles in your torso (the part of your body between your shoulders and hips) that are vital to the creation of your voice. Done properly, support provides your vocal folds with a steady and balanced stream of pressurized air. This air then makes your vocal folds vibrate together and generate sound.

There are 4 main support jobs to master: chest, ribs, the top belly 'magic spot,' and the bottom belly. Precise control of your support system will allow you to not only sing easily and healthily, but can also solve long-standing vocal problems that you may have encountered in the past. It will also prevent future problems, as the use of good support helps protect your vocal folds from harm.

To locate your two bellies, imagine that your abdomen is split in half, with a 'top belly' and a 'bottom belly.' Your top belly is the area between your navel and your sternum. Your bottom belly includes your navel and below.

Here are the four jobs of support for singing:

JOB #1 CHEST: Keep chest comfortably up for singing. Don't let it drop.

JOB #2 RIBS: Keep ribs expanded for singing (back and sides). Don't let them collapse.

JOB #3 TOP BELLY: Your top belly needs to gently firm OUT for singing – specifically on its 'magic spot,' as described in the following exercise. Keep it firmed out for every note you sing.

JOB #4 BOTTOM BELLY: Your bottom belly is going to gradually pull in while you are singing. (Yes, that's the opposite of what your top belly is doing.)

## Exercise for Support

*Chest:* Place one hand on your upper chest. Make a loud 'SH' sound and push UP against your hand.

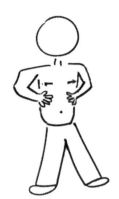

*Ribs:* With your hands on either side of your ribs, (fingers in front and thumbs in back), find your last set of ribs on each side. Now move your hands upwards about two inches. Make a loud, long 'SH' sound. Notice how those ribs may have collapsed? For singing, we want them to stay out. Now try the loud, long 'SH' sound again with your hands remaining on your side ribs and focus on keeping them strongly out.

*Top Belly:* Time to find your top belly's 'magic spot.' It's the spot on your top belly that goes out the *most* when you make a loud 'SH' sound (It's also called the 'epigastrium.') Place 2-3 fingers just below your sternum and say 'SH' loudly. Now move your fingers slightly lower and try it again: 'SH.' Poke around up and down below your sternum until you find the spot that goes out the most. That's your magic spot. It may even feel like a button pushing against your fingers. Do Vocal Exercise #1 ('SH' Pattern) and make your magic spot firm OUT on each sound – especially on the long 'SH' at the end of the pattern. Then relax your belly for breathing. Practice this magic spot exercise daily to strengthen this vital controller of your voice.

*Bottom Belly:* Place your thumb on your navel and the rest of your hand below. Do the 'SH Pattern' again. Your bottom belly should go IN when you    make the sound. The bottom belly then relaxes out completely when you breathe in. Practice the 'SH Pattern' several times loudly.

*Putting it Together:* OK, ready for the combo? Place 3 fingers on your top belly magic spot and the other hand on your bottom belly. Make sure your bellies are relaxed before *you begin. Breathe in and expand your bellies. Now, say 'SH' loudly. You should feel your magic spot firm OUT while your bottom belly pulls IN. (Then, once again, relax your bellies for breathing in.) Now, do Vocal Exercise #1 – monitoring your bellies with your hands. The rule is: work your bellies when making sound; relax them when breathing.*

The goal is to create perfect support for every note you sing – not too little and not too much. Keep your magic spot spongy firm and play with how much support each note requires.

At first, the support jobs may seem like a lot to think about, but by focusing on one job at a time, these actions will soon become second nature to you. We suggest that you master each support job separately (and in the order presented) before doing them in combination.

After you've mastered the 'SH Pattern' Vocal Exercise, continue on with an exercise of your choosing. Consider doing Vocal Exercise 4 or 6 – both are good ones to start with. Remember to first breathe quietly by relaxing your bottom belly, then imagine filling your bellies with air, and finally sing the exercise with strong abdominal support.

Once you've got that down, you can choose a favorite song and practice it while monitoring your belly action with your hands. You'll notice an instant improvement!

No matter what the style – and for every phrase you sing for the rest of your life – use good posture, belly breathing, and the 4 jobs of support. This foundation for great singing will help you achieve control, confidence and consistency!

**KEY POINTS**

Stand up straight, lengthen (but don't stiffen) the back of your neck, hold your chest high, set your ribs wide, and relax your abdomen. Breathe in quietly by relaxing your bottom belly, then imagine filling the belly upwards with air.

When singing, be sure to use the 4 jobs of support: 1) Keep chest up. 2) Keep ribs out. 3) Firm OUT your top belly magic spot. 4) Gradually clutch your bottom belly IN. Posture, breathing, and support are the foundation of great singing and will give you Control, Confidence and Consistency.

# CHAPTER 3
# YOUR SOUND TEAM

In chapter 2, we described the body parts that work similarly for all styles of singing. In this next chapter, we'll describe the body parts that change according to the style that you're singing. These include the tongue, the jaw and lips, the larynx, the soft palate, and the pharynx.

This chapter is intended to help you discover and control these areas. Chapters 6-12 will then explain how to adjust these body parts to create the desired sound for each style.

The following is a diagram of the important parts of sound production:

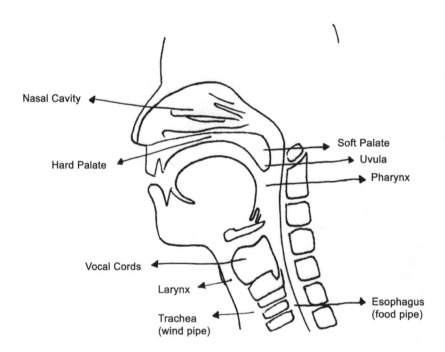

## JAW

The jaw is a large bone that attaches to your head at a joint in front of your ears. It can move in different ways. For vocal styles like opera, you'll want the jaw dropped with a larger mouth opening. For styles like country, you'll use a smaller mouth opening. Also, in some styles the jaw needs to be quite loose, while in other styles the jaw will emulate the firming common in speech.

### Exercise for Jaw

*Watching yourself in a mirror, open and close your jaw. Now, sing a bit from any song and experiment with your jaw opening, noticing how this up-and-down motion changes the sound of your voice.*

## TONGUE

The tip of the tongue will be mostly parked behind your lower teeth (not bunched back). The middle of your tongue can be of varying heights – for example, high (as felt in an 'ee' vowel) or low (as felt in an 'uh' vowel). Eventually, you can gain conscious control over your tongue and be able to lift it higher (which also moves it forward) or keep it flatter. Having this conscious control will help each style sound authentic.

### Exercise for Tongue

*Watching in a mirror, say a long "eeeee." Notice what your tongue does: the tip is against your bottom teeth and the middle is arching high. Now say a long "uuuuuh." Again, notice your tongue. Now, although the tip touches the back of your teeth, the middle and back of your tongue totally flatten out.*

*Next, say a long, held "nee-uh-ee-uh-ee-uh" and give your tongue an up-and-down workout.*

## LARYNX

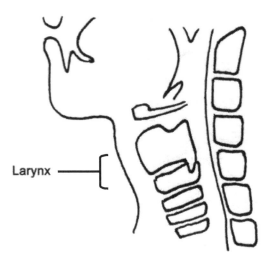

Larynx

Your larynx, also known as your 'voice box,' sits on top of your trachea (wind-pipe).  The left and right vocal folds sit horizontally inside the larynx.  The folds connect right behind the 'Adam's Apple' – the pointy front of the larynx.

Ready to find your larynx?  Place your thumb and index finger on either side of your upper neck.  Swallow.  Feel the bump that moves up and down?  That's your larynx!

You can move your larynx up and down to achieve different sounds.  Try yawning and feel how it lowers.  Now try squeaking and notice how high it can go.  Different styles of music will use different larynx positions.

In general, a higher position is used for country and rock, while a lower position is good for classical and R&B.  When singing styles that sound like high speech or yelling, you may also feel a forward-pulling sensation of the larynx.  We refer to this forward-pulling sensation as ' laryngeal lean.'  Pop, rock, musical theater 'belting,' and country use this 'lean' in their sound.

We will delve into how the larynx moves in each of style chapters, but you can refer to the following diagram for a quick generalization of the relationship between vocal styles and larynx positions.

## Exercise for Larynx

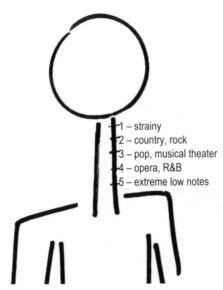

1 – strainy
2 – country, rock
3 – pop, musical theater
4 – opera, R&B
5 – extreme low notes

Let's imagine that you have 5 different larynx positions: #1 is the highest and #5 is the lowest. To demonstrate the positions, stick your hand up in front of your face, palm facing you. Notice how your thumb is on top? We'll call that Larynx Position #1. When you squeak, that's the #1 larynx position. It sounds strainy and doesn't feel good when you sing.

Let's skip for a moment to #3. Say "Hello" in your best, professional voice – that's your #3 position. Now, raise your larynx a little to #2 and you should notice you sound younger. Return for a moment to your #3, home-base position. Then, slightly lower your larynx to #4 and notice that you sound older or sexier. Pull it down even further to the lowest position #5 when you need to amplify your lowest pitches.

A common problem for beginning singers is the natural lifting of the larynx to the #1(highest) position when attempting to sing high notes. This makes your voice sound strainy, shrill, and effortful. Try the following exercise to help you counteract this overlifting. Pull your larynx down to its lowest position (#5) by saying "goh, goh, goh" like you're sobbing. By touching your larynx, you should be able to feel how it lowered dramatically.

Now, let's put it into practice. Sing a phrase with challenging high notes while touching and monitoring your larynx. Attempt to maintain your #3 larynx position by anchoring it downward.

## SOFT PALATE

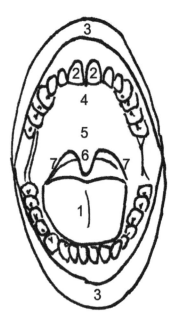

Mouth

1- Tongue
2- Teeth
3 - Lips
4 - Hard Palate
5 - Soft Palate
6 - Uvula
7 - Tonsils

The soft palate is the soft, umbrella-shaped skin behind the hard roof of your mouth (toward the back of your throat). It's important because it can direct sound waves either more through your mouth or more through your nose. You can think of your soft palate as the doorway to your nose. Singers can control to what degree the soft palate hangs down or is lifted.

To discover how your soft palate feels when it's lifted, begin a yawn. The lift you feel in the back during the beginning of the yawn is the feel of your soft palate going up. This lifted position creates a less nasal sound.

If you want a more nasal sound, let your soft palate hang down.

Different styles of music require more or less nasality, as you will see. For now, let's experience moving your soft palate.

### Exercise for Soft Palate

*One great way to tell whether you're singing with your soft palate lifted or not is to make sound while pinching your nose. Close your nostrils with your fingers, then talk through your nose so that you sound funny. That sound results from your soft palate hanging down. Now, with your nose still plugged, say the same thing again while lifting your soft palate. Your voice should sound clear and not-nasal – and that's how you know your soft palate is up!*

## PHARYNX

The pharynx is the space in your throat behind your mouth and your nose, as well as the space above your larynx in your upper neck.  For this book, we are using the word pharynx to mean the space in your upper neck.

The pharynx has three possible positions.  It can be held in a wide position (which is best for classical and R&B singing).  You can also constrict your pharynx (for county and rock singing), or you can keep it neutral (for musical theater, jazz, and pop singing).

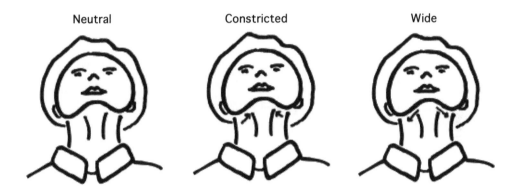

Neutral            Constricted            Wide

### *Exercise for Pharynx*

*Most singers can feel their pharynx with their fingers.  Take your thumb and index finger and place them high on both sides of your upper neck (just below your jaw line on either side of your chin).*

*We've all had the feeling of trying to stifle a laugh in the middle of the library, church or temple, a funeral, or other inappropriate situation.  Try silently laughing right now and see if you can feel how your throat widens.  That's your pharynx in the wide position!  Say a long "ahhh."  Widen your pharynx using the silent laugh and observe the sound difference.*

*Now, relax your pharynx to neutral and say "ahhh" again.  Notice you sound normal.  Finally, constrict the two tiny spots beneath your fingers to create the constricted pharynx position.  Say "ahhh" with this constricted position and notice the sound difference.*

*Play with these three pharynx positions so you can clearly remember the sound and feeling of each.  Important note: When constricting your pharynx, never constrict your vocal folds.  Constricting your pharynx is safe; constricting your vocal folds is dangerous.*

## RESONANCE

To explain resonance, we first must explore the sound created by the vibration of the vocal folds. When vocal folds vibrate, they emit a complex sound (similar to a duck call or a 'raspberry'). This vocal fold sound is actually a mathematical series of pitches called the 'harmonic series.' As that sound travels upward through the spaces of your throat, mouth, and nose (often called your 'resonance chambers'), the sound is actually shaped by those spaces. Certain pitches in the harmonic series are made louder and other pitches are made softer. This array of harmonics creates the character of your voice.

Said another way, your resonance chambers make YOU sound like YOU. Since your head and its holes are unique in the world, so is your voice!

Some of the resonance chambers in your body are able to be consciously controlled – your mouth, for example, can change shape and size. By controlling the size and shape of your resonance chambers, you can change the tone of your voice to match the style you want to sing. Here we'll talk about the three basic bands of resonance that you can adjust: nasality, ring, and brightness.


### Nasality

Nasality is the buzzy sound that results from the sound coming through, well, your nose. Nasality is controlled by the position of your soft palate. As we've seen, to increase nasality, let your soft palate hang down. For less nasality, imagine that you're beginning to yawn so that your soft palate lifts up. Remember, it's not all or nothing. Your soft palate like a dimmer switch -- you can choose more or less nasality as the style suggests.

#### Exercise for Nasality

*Let's compare nasal with not-nasal. Say 'ng' (as in the word 'sing'). That's a completely nasal sound. If you say 'ah' (as in 'hot') with a feeling of delight, you'll have lifted your soft palate and made a not-nasal sound.*


### Ring

Ring is another type of resonance. It's the high, piercing sound that carries your voice. Ring makes you sound louder, clearer, and just plain better. As a result, ring is desirable in all styles of music. You can achieve 'ring' in your sound by making an 'ick face,' as described in the next exercise.

*Exercise for Ring*

*To do the ick face, pull up gently on the sides of your nostrils (as if smelling something stinky but trying not to show it). If your nostrils flare, don't worry. But make sure, when doing the ick face, that you don't wrinkle the bridge of your nose.*

*Ick face may feel weird, but when done correctly, it doesn't look weird. Say "nyee, nyee, nyee" and see if you can amplify the high-end, piercing sound. That's the power of ring!*

## Brightness

Brightness is the final type of resonance. It makes you sound happy and young. To increase the brightness in your sound, just smile and show your upper teeth. For a darker sound, cover your teeth with your lips. You should actually be able to feel brightness as the vibrations on your teeth and hard palate. Try to tune into feeling those vibrations.

*Exercise for Brightness*

*Smile and show several upper teeth. Then say, "I have a bright sound." Now, cover your teeth with your lips and say, "Now I have a darker sound." Done.*

The control of these three resonances – nasality, ring and brightness – will help you create different shades of color with your voice. In the following chapters, we'll discuss how these resonances are used for each particular style of music.

## RESONANCE FEEL

One of the most important indicators of resonance for singers, while actually singing, is the very 'feel' of the voice – where in your face and head you feel tangible vibrations. Often singers can feel vibrations in their nose, mouth, and even scalp. We will be discussing the resonance feel for each vocal style in the coming chapters.

## STYLE SHAPE

We're also suggesting a 'style shape' for each vocal style. It's an easy way to shape your vocal tract and face that combines the many details we present in each chapter into one memorable expression. It can be a quick hint for you when going from style to style.

### KEY POINTS

Your jaw, tongue, larynx, soft palate, and pharynx can all be moved into different positions. The 3 pharynx widths (neutral, constricted, and wide) and 5 vertical larynx positions are important controllers of vocal color.

By learning to isolate and move each of the body parts in this chapter, you will be able to control the sounds and quality of your voice as never before.

Three main resonances of voice are nasality, ring, and brightness. Learning to control these resonances will help you develop into a more expressive singer.

# CHAPTER 4
# INTRODUCTION TO STYLISMS

Not only does each style have its own identifiable sound, but each also features unique expressive vocal effects we call 'stylisms.' Stylisms are like ear candy for the audience, and they help singers add interest and emotion to their songs. Examples of stylisms are vibrato, fry, cry, growl, and runs.

Time to listen to the stylisms provided. You can find and download them easily by logging in at singanything.com. The username is **singer** and the password is **singnow**. Listen carefully and then try them out.

1. Straight Tone
2. Vibrato (wavy tone)
3. Water Vibrato (straight then wavy tone)
4. Cry
5. Creaky Voice
6. Breathy Voice
7. Growl
8. Glides
9. Fry
10. Yodel
11. Swoops
12. Trill
13. Melisma
14. R&B Run
15. Fry Onset
16. Breathy Onset
17. Soft Glottal Click Onset
18. Stops
19. Neighbor Notes
20. R&B Tails (2-note, 3-note, 5-note)
21. Pop Run
22. Scatting
23. Singers' Syllables (adding syllables)
24. Segmenting Long Phrases
25. Rush and Drag
26. Singing on Resonant Consonants: n, m, ng, v, r, z
27. Fall-Offs
28. Shadow Vowels
29. Air Bursts
30. Vertical Laryngeal Changes
31. Pharynx Widths

# CHAPTER 5
# VOCAL TONE

When you choose to sing a style, it's important to sound authentic - not like you're faking it. The main ingredient in sounding real is using the right 'vocal tone.' Vocal tone refers to the particular sound unique to each style.

In classical singing, the vocal tone is a very full, round, and projected sound. Luciano Pavarotti and Joan Sutherland exemplify the classical tone. Musical theater singers, on the other hand, embrace a tone that is full-spectrum, intense, and powerful. Sutton Foster and Idina Menzel are great examples of this. Jazz singers, such as Ella Fitzgerald and Sarah Vaughan, use a great variety of vocal colors in order to express emotion and mood. Pop singers use an accessible, conversational tone that often erupts into a powerful and bright wail. Two examples of performers in this style are Michael Jackson and Kelly Clarkson. Country singers, like Reba McIntyre and Travis Tritt, showcase the dialect and lives of people of the American South. R&B singers, like Aretha Franklin and Usher, utilize the gospel roots of the African-American culture. Rock singers, such as Robert Plant and Pat Benatar, use their voices in extreme ways to communicate youthful rage and sexuality.

All these performers are using resonance to create a specific vocal tone. As you will see, your resonance chambers can be consciously manipulated to achieve the desired vocal tone for any particular style of music. Don't worry, though – you'll still always sound like yourself. Remember, resonance is created in the space between the top of the vocal cords and the end of the lips. As each person is shaped differently, each person will have a unique, individual resonance (or sound) to his/her voice.

As you explore singing different styles, it is important to remember that each vocal style arises from a unique cultural history. Even though our technical approach is meant to help you create an authentic sound related to styles, one truly needs to be surrounded by a style's people and places in order to fully appreciate the depth of its culture and history. So, do some digging.

For each of the next seven chapters, we will first identify the vocal tone of a particular style, and then we'll give you a few examples of singers to listen to. Next, you'll get to practice how to make the physical adjustments that create that vocal tone. Finally, you'll find Vocal Exercises to help you practice making the right sound. We've also included Gina's Style Maps – a visualization what things look and feel like inside your head – and Lisa's Style Shapes – a picture of what your face will look like – for each of the styles.

# CHAPTER 6
# CLASSICAL STYLE

Classical singing is used in opera, operetta, art song, choir, and oratorio (like Handel's <u>Messiah</u>).

The goal of most classical singing is to create a loud and expansive sound. This style is usually sung without the benefit of electronic amplification, so the singer must be loud enough to be heard over a 100-piece orchestra. Try listening to the 'Queen of the Night' aria sung by Joan Sutherland or 'Nessum Dorma' sung by Luciano Pavarotti. Many more songs, performed by masters of the classical style, are listed at <u>singanything.com</u>. Our practice vowel for classical is 'oh.'

## JAW

Your jaw is open and loose with the lips a little puckered and out.

*Drop your jaw and pucker your lips out and away from your teeth. Sing 'oh.' Start on a higher note and slide to a lower one.*

## TONGUE

In order for the voice to sound full and open, keep the tip of your tongue touching the back of the bottom teeth. Keep the remainder of the tongue flat and soft on the floor of the mouth.

*Sing 'oh' with a relaxed, flat tongue, a dropped jaw, and puckered lips.*

## LARYNX

For the classical sound, your larynx is held low (position #4), which results in a good deal of space within the throat. This lowering of the larynx helps create the warm and dark sound associated with classical singing.

*Keeping your tongue, jaw, and lips as above, then lower your larynx by feeling like you're about to throw up (no kidding!) and sing a slidy 'oh.'*

## SOFT PALATE

Classical singing uses very little nasality (like a 1 or a 2 on a scale of 1-10). Lift your soft palate like you're just about to yawn. Feeling yawny reduces nasality.

*With your jaw, tongue, and larynx all in their classical positions, lift your soft palate and sing 'oh.'*

## PHARYNX

In classical singing, your pharynx will be wide.

*Sing that 'oh' again and add the open pharynx by silently laughing. Notice that your tone sounds even more open.*

## RESONANCE

There is very little nasality in classical music, so keep your soft palate up, (feeling yawny). Amplifying your ring is a vital part of the classical sound, so definitely do the ick face as described in Chapter 3. To minimize brightness, keep your lips in an outward pucker.

*Drop your jaw, widen your pharynx, lower your larynx, lift your soft palate, pucker your lips, put some ick on your face, and sing 'oh.' There you go!*

## RESONANCE FEEL

In classical singing, women will feel vibrations in the sinuses, forehead, and head. To facilitate this feeling, the muscles of the upper face must be active. Lift slightly on the sides of your nose, as though something 'icky' smelling is nearby. Your cheeks need to be lifted at all times and your forehead may be lifted slightly, as well. If you look 'snooty' in the mirror, you're probably on the right track. While men should keep that lifted expression on their face, they will feel vibrations in their mouth, throat, and chest, as well.

*Women who sing in a classical style feel much vibration in their upper heads. Men will feel vibrations more in their mouth, throat, and chest. Sing on the 'oh' vowel on higher notes descending to lower notes and try to feel the vibrations in these areas.*

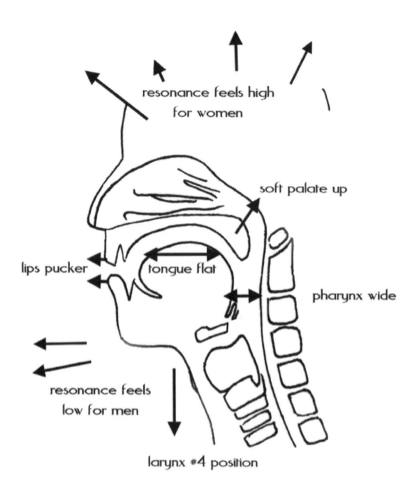

resonance feels high
for women

soft palate up

lips pucker          tongue flat

pharynx wide

resonance feels
low for men

larynx #4 position

## CLASSICAL STYLE MAP

Ready to put it all together? Tongue soft and flat, larynx low, jaw loose, soft palate up, pharynx wide, and cheeks up.  Get ready to use strong abdominal support (ribs out, top belly out, bottom belly in).  Sing a long, slidy 'oh' and enjoy your classical sound.

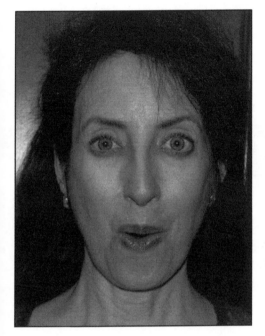

FISH FACE

INSIDE SMILE

## CLASSICAL STYLE SHAPES:
### FISH FACE AND INSIDE SMILE

There are actually two different style shapes common in classical singing. You can use both of them. Women are more likely to use the Inside Smile, and men are more likely to use Fish Face, but it's best to master each. For Fish Face, use puckered lips, dropped jaw, low larynx, lifted soft palate, and look surprised. For Inside Smile, pretend that you're hiding a secret. That means cheeks up, ick face, slight yawn, low larynx, and relaxed tongue.

# INTERPRET IT:  CLASSICAL SONG

## Classical Culture
The roots of classical music extend back in history and include the Medieval period (500-1400), the Renaissance (1400-1600), the Baroque, Classical, and Romantic periods (1600-1910), as well as the 21st Century.  Originating in Western Europe, the classical culture requires great skill, both musically and vocally, and is often considered to be 'high art.'

Beauty of tone is one of the highest goals of classical singing and mastery of the techniques often require many years of study.

## Classical Phrasing and Stylisms
Interpretation of classical music is strict: the singer's task is to follow the composer's written directions.  Dynamic markings – denoting how loud or soft to sing – will be written in the musical notation in most cases.  The rhythms, notes, and tempo are all to be strictly followed, and the singer's artistry must be contained within these structures.

One of the most challenging aspects of classical singing is breath control: the ability to sing long phrases while connecting the vowels in smooth way (called 'legato' singing).

For the vast majority of solo singing in the classical style (with the exception of boy sopranos and early music), Vibrato *(Stylism #2)* is almost always present.  The classical vibrato sounds shimmery, complex, and is more prevalent than in other styles.  Also, the beautiful sound of the voice is paramount, so the clarity of the words may sometimes have to be sacrificed.  And, although your body is working hard to produce the classical sound, it should appear effortless.  That's right: no one will ever know how hard you're working!

There are a few, specific times when a singer needs to add his/her own embellishments in classical music.  One example of these is a Melisma (#13) – an often lengthy, technically challenging melodic line.  Embellishments follow a formula depending on the composer and time period, so consult an expert for further study.

## Variations in Classical Singing
### *Classical:*
Although there are various shades of 'heaviness' and 'lightness' in classical singing, the basic tone remains deep, expansive, and loud.  Wagner or Puccini arias may demand a heavier, more substantial sound, whereas Handel music or French Art Song would require a lighter, more lyrical (pretty) sound.  Use more

belly support and a stronger, uplifted posture when singing the heavier type of classical music.  Allow the lighter classical songs to feel floaty in your head.

*Operetta:*
    The operetta style of singing is a sweeter, lighter version of opera, and it is often performed with a faster vibrato.  A tiny bit of nasality may occasionally be heard in operetta, so lift your soft palate a little less intensely than in opera.  Try adding a Swoop here and there (see Stylism #11).


# EMOTE IT: CLASSICAL SONG

    When singing classical music – especially solo music written after 1600 – imagine yourself as grand, proud, refined, and elegantly passionate.  Stand and emote in a noble manner to express the highest, most civilized values of the human experience.


# LISTEN TO IT:  CLASSICAL SONG

    Some wonderful singers to listen to are Cecilia Bartoli, Renee Fleming, Mario Lanza, Thomas Hampson, and Edita Gruberova.  Here are a few specific suggestions for classical listening.  For more recommended listening, check out singanything.com.
  • Cecilia Bartoli, 'Se Tu M'ami' by Parisotti
  • Mario Lanza, 'Vesti La Giubba' from *Pagliacci*
  • Renee Fleming, 'O Mio Babbino Caro' from *Gianni Schicchi*
  • Placido Domingo, 'Nessum Dorma' from *Turandot*
  • Joan Sutherland, 'Queen of the Night' from *The Magic Flute*


# SING IT: EXERCISES FOR CLASSICAL SINGING

    Exercises, properly done, are important in creating healthy singing habits.  Before you sing songs, it's wise to get comfortable with your new techniques.  To access these on our site, log in with username **singer** and password **singnow**.

Exercise #2:  So

so_____

### Exercise #3: Hung-Oh

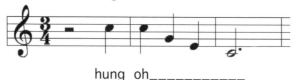

hung oh_____

### Exercise #4: Vah

vah__ vah__ vah__ vah__ vah

### Exercise #5: Eee-Oh

ee__oh__ee_oh____ee__oh__ee__oh__ee__oh__ee_oh____ee__

## SING IT: CLASSICAL SONG

It's time to practice a song. Much classical vocal music is sung in Italian, German, or French, but it's best to start in English. Consider finding a voice instructor who can help you pronounce other languages correctly.

Good beginning classical songs are 'Black is the Color of My True Love's Hair,' 'Drink to Me Only with Thine Eyes,' or the art songs by Roger Quilter based on William Shakespeare texts. Check singanything.com for more suggestions.

Practice the song until you feel really comfortable with it. Listen to as many recorded versions as you can and feel free to imitate elements of your favorites. Plan on at least a dozen or so practice sessions. You will need that many to train your body and to be able to accurately assess your progress.

**KEY POINTS**

Classical singing is used in opera, choirs, early music, and in art songs (such as by Brahms, Faure, Schubert, Schumann, Wolf, and Quilter). It expresses grand passion, ethereal moods, and thunderous power. Classical music has deep historical roots and traditions.

Technically, classical singing demands impressive breath control, steady vibrato, intensely resonant ring, and a command of multiple languages. It employs two different resonator shapes: Fish Face and Inside Smile. Fish Face will make you sound louder and deeper while the Inside Smile results in a more delicate sound. Most classical singers use a combination of the two style shapes.

In classical singing, women sing predominately with a 'heady' sound (as do counter-tenors – men who train to sing with their 'heady' sound). All other men sing in their normal or 'full voice' with an emphasis on depth and power. Be sure to lower your larynx, lift your soft palate, widen your pharynx, and drop your jaw to make the classical sound.

# CHAPTER 7
# MUSICAL THEATER STYLE

In Musical Theater singing, there are two contrasting styles in common use – belting and 'legit.' Belting can be defined as controlled yelling or projected speech. It's bright, intense, and powerful. This is the style most often used in musical theater today, so belting will be the focus of this chapter. Listen to Idina Menzel sing 'Defying Gravity' (from *Wicked*) or Robert Cuccioli sing 'This is the Moment' (from *Jekyll and Hyde*). 'Legit' singing will be discussed later in the chapter. The practice vowel for musical theater belting is 'aa' (as in 'cat').

## JAW

When singing lower notes, your jaw movement will be similar to that of exaggerated talking. However, as you sing higher and carry up your 'talky' sound, your jaw will drop even more and your chin may come forward a little.

*Say 'yaa, yaa, yaa, yaa, yaa, yaa, yaa.' Keep your cheeks up with your lips a little puckered (so you don't tense and spread your lips).*

## TONGUE

For belting, keep the body of your tongue in a high, forward position. By forward position, we mean one where the tip of the tongue is touching the back of the bottom front teeth and the remainder of the tongue is arched high toward the hard palate. Try to keep this forward tongue position for all of your vowels.

*Again in mirror, sing 'yaa, yaa, yaa, yaa, yaa, yaa, yaa' and keep that tongue arched very high in the forward position.*

## LARYNX

In the belting style, your basic larynx position will be a #3. This is the same general height as in speaking. For annoying, ditzy, or young characters, raise your larynx slightly to #2. To sound more romantic or older, lower your larynx to #4. To help you maintain your 'talky' sound as you sing higher, imagine that your larynx is leaning forward as the pitch rises. This feeling is called 'laryngeal lean' (or 'lean' for short).

*Again, in a mirror, sing a bright 'yaa' with a high tongue, and a #3 larynx.*

## SOFT PALATE

Nasality is commonly heard in the musical theater belting sound, so keep your soft palate in a half-lifted position, allowing the sound to resonate in both the nose and the mouth.

*Sing an 'aa' vowel and listen for the buzzy sound of nasality.*

## PHARYNX

The pharynx remains neutral for musical theater singing.

## RESONANCE

Musical Theater showcases strong nasality, ring, and brightness. Keep your soft palate half-lifted for nasality. Show your upper teeth to increase brightness. Use ick face to enhance the ring in your voice.

*Smile with ick face and sing an 'aa' vowel. Listen for the buzz of nasality, and maintain your #3 larynx position.*

## RESONANCE FEEL

The resonance feel of musical theater will vibrate strongly in your nose, sinuses, and teeth.

*Sing the 'aa' vowel strongly and feel the vibrations by placing your fingers on the bridge of your nose.*

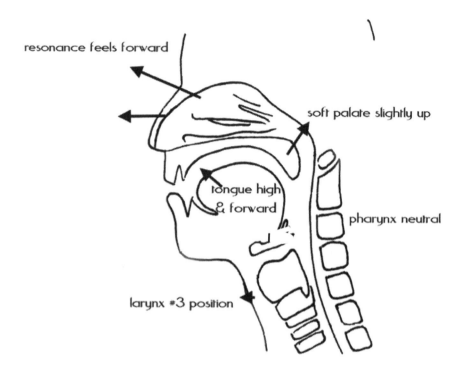

resonance feels forward

soft palate slightly up

tongue high & forward

pharynx neutral

larynx #3 position

## MUSICAL THEATER STYLE MAP

Sing the vowel 'aa' (as in 'cat'). Use the arched tongue position, the larynx in the #3 position, the soft palate in the half-lifted position, the ick face, the smile, and remember your strong abdominal support. Now softly yell 'Yeah, yeah, yeah' and shoot the sound out of your face to the far end of the room.

## MUSICAL THEATER STYLE SHAPE:
### MOLAR MOUTH

For a traditional, brassy belting sound, smile showing upper teeth.      You should feel a pocket of air between your upper molars and the inside of your cheeks.  This is called Molar Mouth.  These pictures show both the front and side views.

# INTERPRET IT: MUSICAL THEATER

## Musical Theater Culture

Musical theater combines story, dance, acting, and singing. Stories highlight political, racial, and sexual tensions in society and between individuals.

## Musical Theater Phrasing and Stylisms

Follow the notes written by the composer relatively closely. Because of the importance on storytelling in musical theater, be sure to emphasize the important words in each phrase and to enunciate all the words with extreme clarity. Feel free to play with the dynamics (the louds and softs) of your songs. Final notes of the phrase can be sung with vibrato or, most often, with a straight tone that then concludes with vibrato. This is called 'Water Vibrato' (Stylism #3).

Other stylisms for Musical Theater singing include Soft Glottal Click Onsets (#17), Stops (#18), Singer's Syllables (#23), and Segmenting Long Phrases (#24).

## Variations in Musical Theater Singing

### 'Legit' Singing:

Many older musicals (pre-1960s) are classified as 'legit' musicals. This style is modeled after classical singing, with a fuller, rounder sound and more use of vibrato. To obtain this sound, lift your soft palate and, for women, sing with a heady sound on your high notes. Use Inside Smile. Examples of legit shows are *The Sound of Music* and *Kiss Me Kate*.

### Rock Musicals:

The line between pop music and musical theater has gotten thinner in recent decades. Musicals like *Rent*, *Footloose*, and *Spring Awakening* use a song style adapted from the pop/rock stage. To sing this style, maintain a musical theater belting technique, but add pop and rock stylisms such as Cry (#4), Breathy Voice (#6), Growl (#7), Neighbor Notes (#19), and Pop Runs (#21). Also, most notes will be sung in Straight Tone (#1).

# EMOTE IT:

Musical theater singing is storytelling. The goal is to create a character and share its emotions with the audience. In traditional shows such as *Oklahoma* or *My Fair Lady*, typical emotions are either sweetly romantic for the leads or comical for the secondary characters.  Modern shows -- especially those that use a belting or pop-rock style – often showcase strong, confident, and sassy traits.

## LISTEN TO IT:  MUSICAL THEATER STYLE

Check out the original queen of belting Ethel Merman.  Then listen to a variety of modern musical theater singers such as Aaron Tvait, Idina Menzel, Stephanie J. Block, Norbert Leo Butz, and Brian D'Arcy James.  For more recommended listening, check out singanything.com.

- Betty Buckley, *Live at Carnegie Hall*
- Linda Eder, 'And So Much More'
- Robert Cuccioli, *Jekyll & Hyde - Broadway version*
- Eden Espinosa, 'Once Upon A Time'
- Idina Menzel, 'Defying Gravity'
- Julie Andrews, *A Little Bit of Broadway* (legit)
- Brian Stokes Mitchell, 'Aldonza' (legit)

## SING IT: EXERCISES FOR MUSICAL THEATER

Remember, it is essential for you to warm-up before each song practice session.  Never begin your warm-up with high volume singing.  Take it easy at first and then gradually increase your volume.  To access these exercises on singanything.com, log in with the username **singer** and the password **singnow**.

Exercise #6:  Bee

bee bee bee bee bee bee bee

Exercise #7: Ng-Aa

Ng_____aa    aa    aa    aa        aa

Exercise #8: Yeah-Woh

yeah  yeah  woh woh woh

Exercise #9:

Can you see the light right ahead of you  showing you the way___

## SING IT: MUSICAL THEATER SONG

Good beginning songs for women are 'Once Upon a Dream' from *Jekyll and Hyde*, 'I'm Not That Girl' from *Wicked,* or 'I Can't Say No' from *Oklahoma*. For guys, consider 'What Do I Need With Love?' from *Thoroughly Modern Millie* and 'Make Them Hear You' from *Ragtime*. Go to **singanything.com** for more suggestions.

Practice the song until you feel like you own it. This means a dozen or more separate practice sessions. The goal is to create muscle memory, so that your body remembers what to do on its own. That way, your brain can focus on creating performance magic.

**KEY POINTS**

Sing like you are speaking.  Remember that in Musical Theater, you are an actor who sings, rather than a singer who acts.  Enunciate very clearly. Use the Molar Mouth shape for the traditional brassy belting sound.  Use strong resonance by increasing ring, brightness and nasality in the exciting parts of the song.  Arch the middle of your tongue, keeping it forward.  To balance your oral and nasal resonance, lift your soft palate a little while sending the sound through your nose.  To help maintain the talky sound as you sing higher, imagine your larynx leaning forward (larngeal lean).

# CHAPTER 8
# JAZZ STYLE

In jazz singing, the goal is to create a mood, as well as to place an individual stamp on the large catalog of songs in the 'Great American Songbook' (the 'standards' typically sung by jazz performers). As a result, jazz vocalists tend to treat their voices like instruments by using a variety of resonances and improvising parts of each performance. This expectation of variance is precisely what makes jazz singing different from the other styles. Listen to Ella Fitzgerald sing 'Hooray for Love' and Billie Holiday's 'Solitude' for two distinct examples of jazz singing. Our vowel for jazz is 'U' as in the words 'should' and 'cook.'

## JAW

For a typical sultry sound, keep your jaw relaxed. Gently pucker your lips while keeping them soft and away from your teeth.

*Pucker your lips like Marilyn Monroe and sing "U."*

## TONGUE

Since text is simple and direct in the jazz style, words will be sung in much the same way as you say them in normal speech. The tongue will remain relaxed (except when you are consciously moving it to play with the sound).

*With slightly puckered lips, sing 'dabadabadabadaba' quickly up and down. Do you notice how flexible and freeing that feels? There's no other style in which you can move your tongue as quickly!*

## LARYNX

Keep your larynx in a #3 position. If however, you want to play with different vocal colors, feel free to move your larynx slightly higher or lower.

*Touching your larynx lightly, pucker your lips, and sing 'dabadabadabadaba'. Now, move your larynx up and down while singing 'dabadabadabadaba,' and listen to how the sound changes when you adjust your larynx position.*

## SOFT PALATE

The positioning of the soft palate can vary in jazz. You can choose between extreme nasality, no nasality, or anywhere in between. (Again, nasality can be felt as the buzzy feeling in your nasal cavity, whereas reduced nasality results in a more open and round sound.)

*Sing an 'U' vowel with soft, puckered lips. Now raise and lower your soft palate to radically shift your degree of nasality.*

## PHARYNX

In jazz singing, you can experiment with all three pharynx positions – neutral, constricted, and wide. But much of the time, use the neutral width.

*The wider the pharynx, the more warm and sultry the tone will be. Experiment by singing a 'U' vowel with a wide pharynx and then with a neutral pharynx. Notice the difference in the sound?*

## RESONANCE

In jazz, extreme resonance choices are acceptable. From dull to ringy, from not-nasal to nasal, or from dark to bright, you can experiment with the full spectrum of vocal resonance.

*Try it...play around with your resonance by moving your soft palate up and down, increasing or relaxing your ick face, and showing or hiding your upper teeth.*

## RESONANCE FEEL

Most jazz singing can be felt as buzzing in the nose, shooting through the hard palate, or vibrating in the forehead.

*Sing an 'U' (as in 'should'). Notice how the feelings of vibration move from mouth to nose to forehead as you ascend in pitch.*

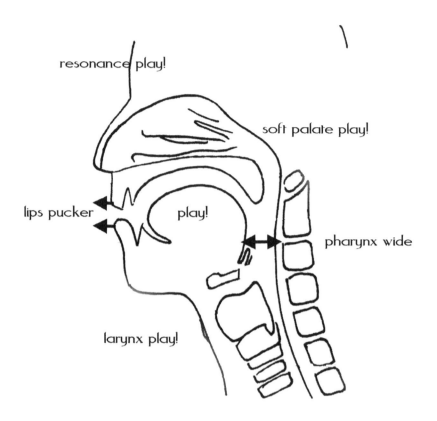

## JAZZ STYLE MAP

This style map will result in a sultry jazz sound. We recommend recording yourself since it is often difficult to accurately hear your voice on the inside as others hear you on the outside. Try a number of different positions with your soft palate, larynx, and pharynx. When you listen back to the recording, listen for tonal changes and their emotional effect.

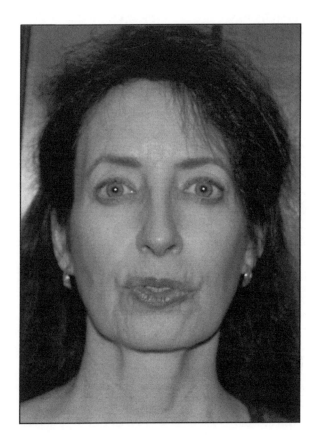

## JAZZ STYLE SHAPE:
### FISH LIPS

Relax your cheeks and gently round and protrude your lips.  This shape results in a sultry jazz sound.

# INTERPRET IT:  JAZZ SONG

## Jazz Culture
From its earliest days in New Orleans (around 1910) to its expansion in the 20th century, jazz has combined African traditions with European popular music. Jazz musicians and singers often possess great technical skill and are masters of improvisation, individual soloing, phrasing, and swing rhythms.  Furthermore, all members of a jazz band interact as equals within the group.  Jazz singers often 'scat' – improvising melodic patterns on syllables (such as 'dah' and 'buh') in imitation of instrumental soloing.

## Jazz Phrasing and Stylisms
Stylistic interpretation is at the heart of jazz performance.  Rhythmic and tempo variations are expected.  One of the hallmarks of rhythmic variation in jazz singing is 'back-phrasing' – coming in slightly later to emphasize a relaxed feel. Back phrasing can be employed throughout a song.  A contrasting rhythmic choice is to 'rush the beat.'  This just means to come in a little early on some of the notes.  Rushing the beat is typically used in faster songs.

There are even more choices in jazz singing!  Within a single musical phrase, you can add a pause or shorten or lengthen the duration of a note.  Believe it or not, you can change the melody, the tempo, and even the words.

Syncopation in rhythm is also a hallmark of jazz.  Simply put, syncopation is the emphasis of beats not usually emphasized.  To syncopate, stress the weak beats of a measure.  So, instead of singing 'ONE two THREE four,' try 'one TWO three FOUR.'

Since jazz requires an individual stamp on a song, changing and adding notes is expected.  There are many techniques for altering or embellishing melody. Here are a few:

- Neighbor Notes: Add nearby notes that are a little higher or  lower than written notes (Stylism #19)
- Add a short sequence of notes (runs) between two written notes or after the last note (Stylism #21)
- Glide between notes (Stylism #8)
- If a melody ascends, when it repeats, make it descend; and vice versa
- Simplify the line - repeat one note instead of going up and down

Phrasing is an important aspect of jazz singing.  Some elements of phrasing include where to breathe; how to stress certain words but not others; and where to be loud or soft.

Here are some phrasing ideas that demonstrated for you on the Stylism tracks found at <u>singanything.com</u>. The numbers refer to the track numbers. To access these, simply log in with username **singer** and password **singnow**.

23. 'Singers' Syllables' – Add a syllable to the following words:
CLoud, CRaving, THrill, Realize, Glad, GReat, Blow, Black

24. Segmenting phrases 'Don't you know that I love you' into chunks
'Don't you / know that I / love you'

25. Jazz Tempo Changes: Rush and Drag - Early entrances and late entrances are permitted. If you begin late, you might want to then rush to the end of the phrase. Ex: 'Now—you say you're sorry.'

26. Certain consonants can be held out in jazz: n, m, ng, v, l, r and z. Example: 'My man, I love him. His singing stirs me'

27. Fall-Offs

28. Shadow Vowels

29. Air Bursts

30. Vertical Laryngeal Changes

Another common stylism in jazz singing is 'Water Vibrato' (Stylism #3). To create Water Vibrato, just hold a Straight Tone (#1) and then add Vibrato at the end of the tone (#2). This is especially effective on the last word of the phrase. For starting a phrase, try a Fry (#9). Other sounds typical of jazz singing are Breathy Voice (#6), Glides (#8), and Soft Glottal Click Onsets (#17).

Improvisation (making it up as you go along) is a specialty of many – though by no means all – jazz singers. At its most extreme and exciting, this includes vocal 'scatting.' Scatting uses random, made-up syllables to create a vocal line similar to instrumentalists' solos. Serious jazz singers should study and sing along with solos by such greats as Louis Armstrong, Charlie Parker, and Dizzy Gillespie to get good at this amazing vocal art. Check out recordings of Ella Fitzgerald's 'Cotton Tail' or 'How High the Moon' to hear great examples of scatting. This is an advanced technique, and it's best to study or coach with a teacher who specializes in jazz.


## Variations in Jazz

### Swing Jazz

A popular jazz singing style, often heard in Big Band ensembles, is sometimes referred to as 'swing jazz.' This music often has a fast tempo and a triplet feel.

This vocal style requires a brighter sound – best achieved by smiling and showing 6-10 upper teeth.

Of all the vocal styles discussed in this book, jazz exhibits a larger range of tonal variations than any other.  As a result, you can sing a song simply...or you can explore ringy/dull, bright/dark, high-larynx/low-larynx, nasal/not-nasal, clear/breathy sounds all within one song.


## EMOTE IT:

The expressive power of jazz singing arises more from the mood rather than the story.  Moods tend to be reflective and romantic – based on the wisdom gleaned from years of real-life experience.  Tales of love and heartbreak are told from a mature point of view.


## LISTEN TO IT:  JAZZ SONG

Some wonderful singers to listen to are Ella Fitzgerald, Sarah Vaughn, Carmen McRae, Shirley Horn, Joe Williams, Mel Torme, Louis Armstrong, Jon Hendricks, George Benson, Nina Simone, and Jane Monheit.  Here is a list of specific tracks for jazz listening.  For more recommended listening, check out the website singanything.com.

- Ella Fitzgerald, *The Best of Ella Fitzgerald: the First Lady of Song*
- Jane Monheit 'Never Neverland' and 'Come Dream with Me'
- Jon Hendricks & Friends, 'Freddie Freeloader'
- Michael Feinstein, *Romance on Film, Romance on Broadway*
- Sarah Vaughn, *The Divine Sarah Vaughn: The Columbia Years*


## SING IT: EXERCISES FOR JAZZ SINGING

Remember: before practicing your songs, you'll need to first warm-up your voice.  To access these on singanything.com, log in with username **singer** and password **singnow**.  Here's your list of warm-ups for jazz:

Exercise #10:  Moo

moo__ moo__ moo__ moo__ moo

## Exercise #11: I Know

I    know   I know I know I   know

## Exercise #12: Daa Buh Dup Buh Doo Bee

daa___ buh dup__ buh doo__ bee

## Exercise #13: Whenever Night Has Come

Whenever night has come we'll   take  a  ride

# SING IT: JAZZ SONG

It's time to practice a song. We suggest beginning with easy jazz songs such as 'Girl from Ipanema,' 'Don't Get Around Much Anymore,' and 'All the Way.' Check out the website singanything.com for more suggestions.

Listen to many different recordings of the jazz songs you choose to sing. Notice how each singer makes unique choices – changing the key, tempo, phrasing, melody, and sometimes even the lyrics. Get inspired by the jazz greats before putting your own specific spin on a song. In jazz, you may never sing the same song the same way twice...and that's a good thing!

---

**KEY POINTS**

Remember to experiment when singing jazz. Have fun creating your own masterpiece by playing with the melody, rhythms, and tonal colors of your voice. To get started, use Fish Lips for the sultry sound or a simple smile for the swingy jazz sound. Study the jazz greats before putting your individual stamp on a song. Then go, be fearless.

---

# CHAPTER 9
# POP STYLE

Of all the singing styles, pop is the most accessible to the general public. Pop is, of course, short for 'popular'! It can be fun, uplifting, or just make you want to dance. In pop, your sound will often begin like effortless conversation. Then it will inspire awe as you erupt into a powerful and bright wail. Great examples of pop singing are 'Because of You' by Kelly Clarkson and 'Thriller' by Michael Jackson. The practice vowel for pop singing is 'ee' as in the word 'street.'

## JAW

As pop singing is conversational, your jaw will move up and down like in normal speech. However, as you start to wail up high, your jaw will drop much more.

*Sing 'ee' on a long, low note with a relaxed jaw. Then, sing 'ee' on long, high note. Drop your jaw to help create a loud, full tone.*

## TONGUE

Raise the middle of your tongue into an arched position to achieve a brighter sound.

*Sing a note on 'ee' with a relaxed tongue. Now notice how you can increase the brightness of the tone by arching the middle of your tongue up higher while keeping the tip of the tongue down and touching the back of the bottom teeth. Arching your tongue this way is also a great trick to making your lower notes sound louder and clearer.*

## LARYNX

Use a #3 larynx position for pop singing since it emulates the sound of speech. For a younger or more angsty sound, raise your larynx slightly to #2.

*Sing 'ee' on a comfortably low note with a loose jaw and a highly arched tongue. Feel your larynx with your fingers to make sure it stays in your #3 position. Keep touching your larynx while you cry out 'yeah' on a high note. Make sure that larynx stays relatively still. If it pops up, drop your jaw more and try again.*

## SOFT PALATE

The soft palate will be moderately lifted to create a slightly nasal sound.

*Sing the 'ee' with your nose plugged (as described in chapter 3) to make sure that your soft palate is in the correct half-lifted position for pop singing.*


## PHARYNX

Use a neutral pharynx for pop singing.


## RESONANCE

Pop singing typically has dullish resonance in the verses and more ring in the choruses. So save your ick face for the higher, louder, and more exciting parts of the song. A bright tone is also common in pop singing – achieve that by showing as many as 8 upper teeth, especially if the song is a happy one. Aim for medium nasality with a half-lifted soft palate.

*Sing the 'ee' sound with the soft palate half-lifted, #3 larynx, neutral pharynx, and a smile showing upper teeth for brightness. Now, add ick face to the sound to hear the added ring. Could you hear it?*


## RESONANCE FEEL

In the softer verses of a pop song, you may feel vibration on the ridge behind your front teeth. The verses may also use a softer, breathier sound. When singing this way, you'll feel fewer vibrations in your face. During your more powerful, resonant choruses, though, expect to feel intense vibrations in your nose and the front of your face.

*Smile, support, and sing away on an 'ee' sound.*

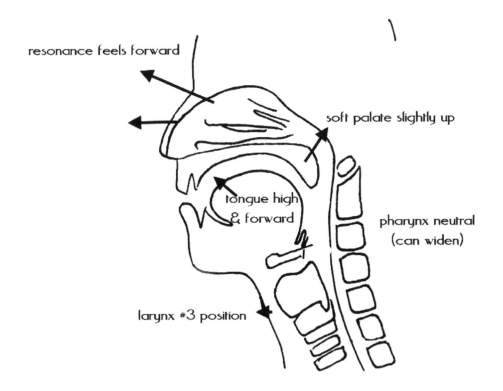

resonance feels forward

soft palate slightly up

tongue high & forward

pharynx neutral (can widen)

larynx #3 position

## POP STYLE MAP

Time to make a pop wailing sound – let's put it all together on the vowel 'ee': mid-tongue arched up, #3 larynx, soft palate slightly up, cheeks raised, and smile with upper teeth showing.  Now, sing a loud 'ee' with strong abdominal support. Feel those intense vibrations in your teeth, hard palate, and nose?

## POP STYLE SHAPE:
### SMILE

Just smile with 4-10 upper teeth showing.
Don't overextend the spread of your lips.

# INTERPRET IT: POP SONG

## Pop Culture

Popular music is intended to be simple, enjoyable, and often danceable. Contemporary pop songs are written by and for young people with lyrics focusing on dating, young love, having fun, and expressing teenage angst (but in a safe way). Some successful pop singers have limited vocal range and talent but still can achieve fame based on their looks or the 'catchiness' of their songs.

## Pop Phrasing and Stylisms

Many pop singers are also songwriters who showcase their unique skills or idiosyncrasies in their songs. Most contemporary pop music in the US is now actually a blend of pop with R&B, rock, or country styles. R&B, in particular, with its embellishing runs (quickly-sung, added notes on 'yeah' or 'oh'), has now become part of mainstream pop singing. These runs, also known as riffs and licks, are generally employed at the beginnings or ends of phrases. Christina Aguilera and Mariah Carey use these ornamental runs often.

Vibrato (Stylism #2) - especially Water Vibrato (#3) – is common on long, held notes, particularly in the chorus part of songs. But a Straight Tone (#1) is often used in the 'talkier' verses. Enunciation should be somewhat clear, but not overemphasized like in musical theater. When it comes to the 'beat,' keep it simple - stay right on it - not rushing or dragging as in jazz.

There are several types of onsets used in pop singing. An onset is the action your vocal folds make when beginning a word that starts with a vowel (like in the word "at"). Try a Fry Onset (#15), a Breathy Onset (#16), or a Soft Glottal Click (#17). For extra expressivity, add a Cry (#4) and a Vocal Fry (#9) to your song. You can even throw in Neighbor Notes (#19), a Pop Run (#21), or an R&B Run (#14).

## Variations in Pop Music

Many pop singers borrow from other styles to create combinations such as pop/rock, pop/country, or pop/R&B. Although we will be covering those styles in depth in the coming chapters, we can generally say that for an R&B influence (like in Adele's songs), you just widen your pharynx and lower your larynx. To add a rock influence (like in Pink's songs), put your mouth into more of a square and raise your larynx slightly. And if you want to go a little country (as in Faith Hill's songs), drop your soft palate to add nasality and constrict your pharynx slightly.

## EMOTE IT:

Pop lyrics convey a broad array of thoughts and topics, but at the top of the list would have be love – as in 'I love you,' 'Don't leave me,' 'I can't live without you,' 'I hate you,' and 'I'm fine without you.' There's a simplicity, earnestness, and even intensity to pop feelings. Everything feels really dramatic and intense in a pop song – like your life depends on expressing your feelings. Dance songs are often highly sexual, celebratory, or create a feeling of power and optimism.

## LISTEN TO IT:  POP SONG

Some wonderful singers to listen to are Richard Marx, Alanis Morrissette, Paul McCartney, Karen Carpenter, Lady Gaga, and Katy Perry. Here's some suggested listening for the pop style. For more recommended listening, check out the website singanything.com.
- Madonna, 'Music'
- Beatles *Sgt. Pepper's Lonely Hearts Club Band* & *Abbey Road*
- Kelly Clarkson, 'I Do Not Hook Up'
- Katy Perry, 'Firework'
- Robbie Williams, 'Free'

## SING IT: EXERCISES FOR POP SINGING

For access to these exercises, log in at **singanything.com** with username **singer** and password **singnow**. Begin by stretching your body and practicing the 'sh' pattern for abdominal support. Next, sing the following exercises:

Exercise #14:  Mee-May

mee may  mee  may     mee

Exercise #15: Naa

naa naa naa naa naa naa naa naa naa naa

## Exercise #16: Come On, Let's Go

Come on let's go__ go__ go_____

## Exercise #17: You Mean Everything To Me

You mean_ ev'rything    ev' ry thing_ to_ me_____

## SING IT: POP SONG

Now, you're ready to practice a song. Try 'Unwritten' by Natasha Bedingfield or 'Blackbird' by The Beatles. More suggestions are at singanything.com.

Begin your practice by listening carefully to the vocalist's performance. Which larynx position do you hear? Do you hear brightness, ring, and/or nasality? How airy or clean is their tone? Where do the singers add vibrato? Once you hear the details clearly, then jump in and practice. The more you practice, the better you will get at not only that song, but at singing in general.

**KEY POINTS**

For the pop style, feel like you're speaking on pitch for the verses and wail on the choruses. Keep your larynx at the #3 position and your pharynx neutral. Use brightness throughout the song by using that high, arched tongue. Add nasality and ring for the choruses. Don't over-enunciate your diction and sing right on the beat. Using the many pop stylisms we mentioned will help you create an expressive vocal performance.

# CHAPTER 10
# COUNTRY STYLE

Country songs are great stories wrapped in a unique, Southern (American) sound. They can be simple and quiet or intense and loud. Listen to 'Bless the Broken Road' by Rascal Flatts and 'Cowboy Casanova' by Carrie Underwood. The practice vowel for country singing is 'oo' as in the word 'mood.'

## JAW

Although country singing is conversational – like pop singing – your jaw action will be more limited. Try to keep your upper teeth fairly close to your bottom teeth, so that only the width of one fingertip can be inserted between your front teeth. Pucker your lips forward tightly.

*Sing 'oo' on a long tone with a slightly closed jaw.*

## TONGUE

Country singing calls for a unique tongue action. You can rest your tongue tip against your bottom teeth, but if you pull the tip **back**, away from your lower teeth (called a 'retracted tip'), you'll sound even more twangy. Also, be sure to feel the sides of your tongue touching your upper back molars.

*Now sing an 'oo' with a Southern accent – tongue tip retracted and the sides of your tongue touching upper back molars. Sounds more country, right?*

## LARYNX

Country singing often uses a higher larynx position – a #2 to be exact. This makes the sound a little more whiny.

*Sing 'oo' on a low note with your new tongue position and raise your larynx slightly. If you're feeling strain on your vocal folds in this position, then your larynx is too high. Aim for a slightly raised larynx, but be sure your vocal folds still feel comfortable.*

## SOFT PALATE

The soft palate will be dropped and hanging to create an intensely nasal sound.

*Sing the 'oo' with the slightly lifted larynx, and then drop your soft palate. Notice how your tone gets more nasal and buzzy.*

## PHARYNX

The pharynx in country singing is constricted. Make sure you don't constrict your vocal folds, though. You'll just be constricting the upper throat below your jaw line near your chin, but ABOVE your larynx. The constricted pharynx increases the nasal sound.

*Sing the 'oo' with your soft palate dropped and your larynx slightly raised. Pucker your lips. Now squish your upper throat (pharynx) in sideways just a little. Feel the space in your throat narrow? If your vocal folds feel tense or squeezed, relax everything and start again, only constricting the pharynx slightly, below your jaw line.*

## RESONANCE

Nasality is the predominant resonance in country singing. Use more nasality for a kickin' song and less nasality for a romantic one. Use a minimum of brightness by keeping your lips in front of your teeth and use ick face to add ring – especially in the choruses of the song.

## RESONANCE FEEL

People expect the country style to be very nasal and sung with a Southern American accent. You will feel intense vibrations in your nose and front portion of your hard palate.

*Sing the vowel 'oo.' Then sing the words 'Take Me Home' with a Southern accent, retracted tongue tip, and teeth very slightly apart. Where do **you** feel the vibrations?*

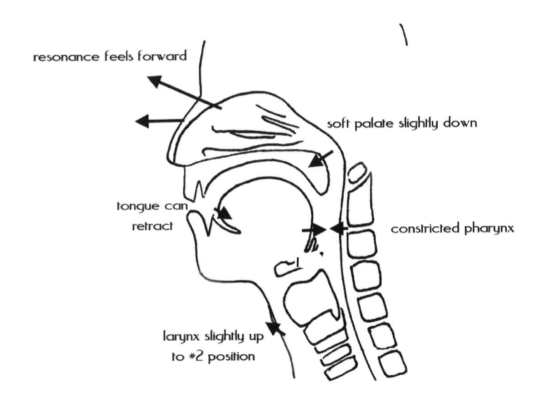

resonance feels forward

soft palate slightly down

tongue can retract

constricted pharynx

larynx slightly up to #2 position

## COUNTRY STYLE MAP

Pucker your lips a little, raise your larynx to a #2 position, constrict your pharynx, and drop your soft palate. Sing a long, loud, nasal 'oo' and feel intense vibrations inside your nose and mouth. If you are feeling brave, retract your tongue tip a little and see what happens!

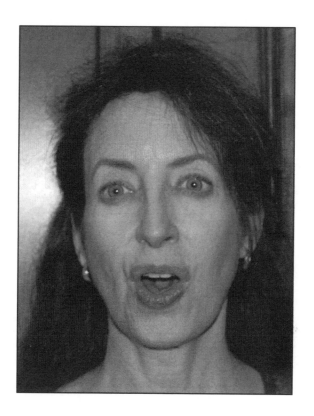

## COUNTRY STYLE SHAPE:
### FULL TUBE

The style shape for country singing is called the Full Tube.
This shape requires puckered lips, narrow pharynx, raised larynx, dropped soft palate and the feeling that your tonsils are touching.

# INTERPRET IT:  COUNTRY SONG

## Country Culture
   This American musical style has its roots in the music of the Western cowboy and in Southeastern folk music.  Often 'twangy' sounding, this music uses electric and acoustic instrumentation that includes mandolins, fiddles, and steel guitars.  Once a niche market, country music has become mainstream and is now one of the most popular music forms in the US.

## Country Phrasing and Stylisms
   Generally a country song is sung the way that it is written.  The phasing is short and conversational for the most part – until you get to wail out those long high notes.  Say your words clearly, but minimize the amount of vibrato that you use.  Add a little Cry (Stylism #4) to your voice for sad, heart-wrenching songs.  Look fairly relaxed, too – like it's easy.  For onsets, consider putting a little baby Growl (#7) at the beginning of a line/phrase.  Play with Yodels (#10) or Frys (#9) at the beginning of words.

## Variations in Country Music
   There are a number of songs and artists (like Carrie Underwood and Taylor Swift) who sing on the boundary of pop and country.  When singing this 'crossover country' style, lift your soft palate a little to be less nasal and let your larynx drop into a #3 position for a more open sound.

# EMOTE IT:
   Country lyrics are usually simple, honest and direct.  In addition to songs about mature love and its up-and-downs, topics also touch on home, work, family, and the glories of Southern life.  Approach the country style with quiet dignity and a strong, straightforward attitude.

# LISTEN TO IT:  COUNTRY SONG
   Here is a list of specific tracks for country listening.  For more recommended listening, check out singanything.com.
- Travis Tritt, *Greatest Hits from the Beginning*
- LeAnn Rimes, 'Blue'
- Alan Jackson, *The Greatest Hits Collection*
- Garth Brooks, *No Fences* (country pop)

- Taylor Swift, 'Love Story'
- Dixie Chicks, 'Not Ready to Make Nice'

## SING IT: EXERCISES FOR COUNTRY SINGING

Begin by stretching your body. Stand with good singing posture and then warm up your belly by doing the 'sh' pattern (*Exercise #1*). After you've done the following exercises, you'll be ready to practice your song. Access these exercises at singanything.com with username **singer** and password **singnow**.

Exercise #18: Hohn

hohn_____

Exercise #19: Nay

nay  nay  nay  nay   nay  nay_   nay

Exercise #20: Come on Down to a Place I Know

Come  on  down  to  a   place I ___  know_

Exercise #21: Where Can I Go

Where can I go___ where I'd never stop be-lieve-in  at all_____

## SING IT: COUNTRY SONG

Time to practice a song!  Try 'Landslide' by the Dixie Chicks or 'When You Say Nothing at All' by Keith Whitley.  You'll find more song suggestions at singanything.com.

Practice your song until it feels like a part of you.  Remember that practice doesn't make perfect, practice makes **permanent**.  So, practice with attention to detail.  After you've developed dependable muscle memory, you'll be better able to create magical performances.

**KEY POINTS**

Remember to use the Full Tube shape when singing in the country style. Lower your soft palate, lift your larynx to the #2 position, imagine that your tonsils are touching, and use the constricted pharynx position. Be sure to never squeeze your vocal folds. Send the vibrations straight through your nose. Sing with a Southern drawl to really sell the style!

# CHAPTER 11
# R&B STYLE

R&B stands for Rhythm & Blues – a group of African-American vocal styles including soul, blues, spirituals, gospel, and hip-hop.  R&B is powerfully emotional and uses the largest possible range of notes, volume, and personal emotion. Listen to Stevie Wonder's 'Always' and Beyonce's 'Love on Top.'  The practice vowel for R&B singing is a dark 'aah' as in the word 'yeah.'

## JAW

Your jaw is going to loose and dropped for R&B music.

*Sing 'aah' on a long tone and let your lower jaw be dropped and limp – as though the dentist just shot you with Novocain.*

## TONGUE

Your tongue should be wide and fat.  It should spread to the inside of your lower molars.

*Open your jaw and sing the dark 'aah.'  Widen your tongue and notice how the sound deepens.*

## LARYNX

Though many R&B singers use a #3 larynx position, we recommend singing by lowering your larynx to the #4 position. This results in a much deeper, warmer sound.

*Sing 'aah' with a loose, dropped jaw and a fat, wide tongue.  Drop your larynx a little and notice how the tone is affected.*

## SOFT PALATE

The soft palate will be moderately dropped to create a naturally nasal sound.

*Sing a dark 'aah' with slight nasality and feel the vibrations on your nose and teeth.*

## PHARYNX

The pharynx in R&B singing is wide.  This adds a sultry, full sound to your tone.

*With your soft palate and jaw slightly dropped, your larynx lowered to #4 position, and your tongue wide and flat, sing an 'aah' with a wide pharynx.  Listen to the fullness that you've just created!*

## RESONANCE

Your lips will be relaxed for R&B singing – with no teeth showing.  This will reduce the brightness of your tone.  Aim for noticeable nasality by dropping your soft palate.  Use ick face to amplify ring for the louder and higher sections.

## RESONANCE FEEL

Aim for a powerful, full sound for R&B.  Enjoy the feeling of intense vibrations just about everywhere in your face!

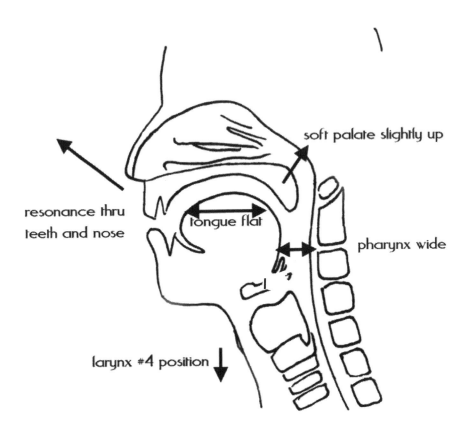

resonance thru
teeth and nose

soft palate slightly up

tongue flat

pharynx wide

larynx #4 position

## R&B STYLE MAP

With your tongue wide and flat, lower your larynx to #4, drop your soft palate slightly, and widen your pharynx. Get ready to use strong abdominal support and the ick face for the choruses. Sing a projected, long 'aah' (dark aa) on a high wail and experience the soulful but intense sound.

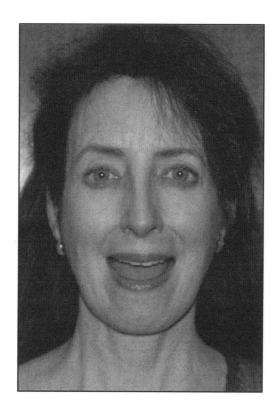

## R&B STYLE SHAPE:
## WATER-IN-THE-MOUTH

The resonator shape for R&B is 'water-in-the-mouth.' With your tongue fat and wide, pull your jaw down within the skin of your face as if you are trying to keep a mouthful of water from dripping out. The upper portion of your face looks like a wide smile with no teeth showing.

## INTERPRET IT:  R&B SONG

### R&B Culture

Rhythm & Blues can be thought of as a broad category of musical styles, created originally by and for African-Americans.  R&B has recently merged with pop music to become perhaps the most popular commercial style in the world. R&B includes soul, gospel (religious music from which R&B originated), adult contemporary, funk, blues, rap, and hip-hop.

### R&B Phrasing and Stylisms

R&B ornaments include R&B Tails (Stylism #20), Glides (slides) between notes (#8), Creaky Voice (#5), and Fry (#9).  R&B Runs (#14), also known as riffs or licks, are unique to this style and are important contributions.  Runs are ornamental lines of quickly-sung notes on syllables such as 'yeah' or 'oh'.  Sing along with Christina Aguilera and Mariah Carey on your path to mastering these. Vibrato (#2) – especially Water-Vibrato (#3) – is used commonly for sustained notes, particularly in the chorus.  Straight Tone (#1) is used in the 'talkier' verses.

### Variations in R&B Music

Artists like Adele live on the edge between pop and R&B styles.  To combine pop and R&B, raise your larynx to the #3 position, arch your tongue to brighten your tone, and smile (showing a few upper teeth) to sound more conversational.

## EMOTE IT:

Expression of emotion can vary between men and women in this style. Typically in R&B, women are assertive, even dominating.  Moods can shift quickly from sweet to dramatic by singing rapid changes in tone, loudness, and range. Men are often more sensitive in R&B songs – pledging to be faithful or worthy of a woman's love.  R&B is sensual for both, so free body movement is encouraged. Ecstasy, religious or sexual, is often expressed in the R&B style.

## LISTEN TO IT:  R&B SONGS

Here are a few R&B songs to listen to.  For more recommended listening, check out the website singanything.com.

- Etta James, 'Church Bells'
- Aretha Franklin, *The Very Best of Aretha Franklin, Vol.1*
- Whitney Houston 'I'm Your Baby Tonight,' *Whitney Houston*
- Stevie Wonder, *Greatest Hits*
- Beyonce, 'Irreplaceable'
- Marvin Gaye, 'Mercy Mercy Me'

## SING IT: EXERCISES FOR R&B SINGING

Remember, always warm-up and do some exercises to get your voice ready to sing.  Twenty minutes of this warm-up is plenty.  You can access these exercises by logging into singanything.com with the username **singer** and the password **singnow**.

Exercise #22: Yeah

yeah_____

Exercise #23:  Woh

woh_ woh_ woh_____

Exercise #24:  Loving You Tonight

Lov__ in you_ to night___

## Exercise #25: You're the One for Me

I know that u r the 1 for me_____ yeah_____

## SING IT: R&B SONG

It's time to practice a song. Try 'At Last' by Etta James or 'Ain't Too Proud to Beg' by the Temptations. You'll find more practice song ideas at singanything.com.

When you change the shape of your resonators (throat, mouth, and nose) to new and different shapes, you may feel that the sound is strange and artificial. But in fact, you may actually be making the correct sound! Listen to recordings of R&B singers, and notice any R&B runs that you hear. The more you listen and imitate the greats, the more naturally you will be able to create your own improvisations.

**KEY POINTS**

The resonator shape 'Water-in-the-Mouth' is a great way to produce the R&B sound quickly and efficiently. Achieve a deep sound by lowering your larynx and widening your pharynx. For phrasing, slide up and down between the notes of the melody. Also, the beat rules in R&B. Practice clapping **ON** the beat and **AFTER** the beat (also known as 'laying back on the beat'), so your singing does not float OVER the beat, but is rather reacting to the power of it.

# CHAPTER 12
# ROCK STYLE

Rock singing is sexy, loud, and aggressive. It's a high-octane vocal style that demands energy and stamina. Listen to Led Zeppelin's 'Whole Lotta Love' and Fergie's 'Barracuda.' The practice vowel for rock is 'ay' as in 'hey.'

## JAW

Aim for a large open mouth with lips protruding in a square shape.

*Sing 'ay' on a long high note. Drop your jaw to help project your voice.*

## TONGUE

While keeping the tip of your tongue against your bottom teeth, arch the middle part of your tongue. This action will add brightness to your sound.

*Drop your jaw and sing an 'ay' with your tongue arched in the middle.*

## LARYNX

Your larynx position for rock singing will be #3 or slightly raised to #2. The #2 position helps to create that intense, searing sound.

*Sing 'ay' with squared lips and tongue arched. Let your larynx lift up to a #2 position and hear how the sound becomes more of a squeal. If you feel strainy, check that your larynx has stayed at a #2 or #3...and has not crept up to a #1.*

## SOFT PALATE

Let your soft palate hang a bit to create a slightly nasal sound.

*Sing the 'ay' vowel with a slightly dropped soft palate. Combine this with your arched tongue, larynx position #2 or #3, and square lips. Hear the buzz that nasality creates.*

## PHARYNX

Use the constricted pharynx for upbeat rock singing.  For ballads, a neutral pharynx is suggested.

*Sing 'ay' with your jaw and soft palate dropped, lips squared, tongue arched, and larynx raised to the #2 position.  Now, constrict your pharynx just below your jaw line to create that intense rock sound.*

## RESONANCE

Successful rock singers use a lot of resonance to create a wall of sound.  Increasing resonance is one of the keys to preventing vocal fold damage in professional rock singers.  Because strong ring, brightness, and nasality give the illusion of great power and projection, rock singers can minimize vocal fold work and still get the job done by exploiting these.

## RESONANCE FEEL

Rock singing is known for its extreme sound.  Expect to feel intense vibrations in your chest, neck, mouth, nose, teeth, and the front of your face.

*Do your ick face, square your lips, and a raise your larynx to #2.  Constrict your pharynx and wail powerfully on an 'ay' vowel using strong support (chest up, ribs out, top belly out, bottom belly in).*

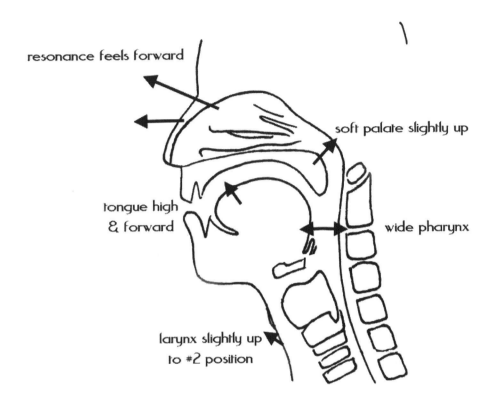

resonance feels forward

soft palate slightly up

tongue high
& forward

wide pharynx

larynx slightly up
to #2 position

## ROCK STYLE MAP

Arch your tongue and lift larynx a little up to #2, square your lips, drop your soft palate slightly, and constrict your pharynx. Using strong abdominal support, project the vowel 'ay' on a high wail and feel intense vibrations on your face. Gnarly.

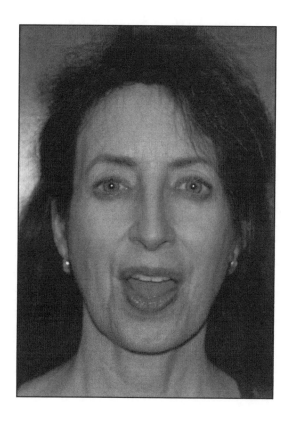

## ROCK STYLE SHAPE:
### SQUARE MOUTH

The resonance shape for rock is the Square Mouth.  Lips will
be protruding out in a square shape and your tongue will be in an
'aa' (as in 'cat') shape.

# INTERPRET IT:  ROCK SONG

## Rock Culture
Rock music began as 'rock and roll' – a combination of West African music and European instrumentation in the 1950s.  It's usually a loud, amplified style featuring drums, electric bass, and electric guitar.  Topics express the thoughts, feelings, and interests of teen culture: cars, romance, sex, drugs, and political activism.

## Rock Phrasing and Stylisms
The rhythm of rock music is typically a strong, simple 4/4, and singers should approach the rhythm in a precise, hard-hitting way.  Choruses tend to be high in pitch and high in volume requiring real 'vocal chops' (technical ability).

Fry Onsets (Stylism #15) and Glides (#8) are used extensively at the beginning of phrases.  Growls (#7) and Creaky Voice (#5) are extreme vocal effects that should be used sparingly in most rock songs.  For some drama at the end of your phrase, throw in a Shadow Vowel (#28).  Also, use Straight Tone (#1) almost always.

## Variations in Rock Music
Rock music has many variations.  Grunge, heavy metal, punk, and screamo are just a few.  These extreme vocal styles are less like singing and more like primal screaming.  So, increase the use of Growls (#7) and Creaky Voice (#5).  If you want to pursue these more radical rock styles, consult with a rock singing specialist.

# EMOTE IT:

To really pull off the rock style, you will need to access your aggressive, 'yang' energy.  Feel wild and dangerous.  Embrace fearlessness, aggression, and raw sexuality.  Even when singing softly, feel powerful and be committed to creating an intense performance.  Rock singers are expected to dominate the audience.

## LISTEN TO IT:  ROCK SONGS

Check these out...and more suggestions at singanything.com:
- Led Zeppelin, 'Whole Lotta Love'
- Scorpions, 'Rock You LIke a Hurricane'
- Pat Benatar, 'Hit Me With Your Best Shot'
- Goo-Goo Dolls, 'Iris'
- Fergie, 'Barracuda'
- Pink, 'Sober'
- Steelheart, 'She's Gone'

## SING IT:  EXERCISES FOR ROCK SINGING

Never jump into a rock song without adequate vocal warm-up.  Always start softly and at a low pitch before you sing high, loud notes.  Here are some great exercises to get your voice ready to sing rock songs.  To access these, log into **singanything.com** with username **singer** and password **singnow**.

### Exercise #26: Yeah

yeah  yeah  yeah  yeah  yeah

### Exercise #27: Naa

naa    naa    naa    naa

### Exercise #28: Get Up and Go

get up and go

Exercise #29: Don't Go There

don't__ go__ there_____    don't_ go there

## SING IT: ROCK SONG

Two good songs for guys to begin with are 'Twist and Shout' by the Beatles or 'I Can't Get No Satisfaction' by the Rolling Stones.  For the ladies, try 'Heartbreaker' by Pat Benatar or 'Come to My Window' by Melissa Etheridge. Check out singanything.com for more suggestions.

Each time you practice your song, add something new, different, or courageous.  Try to use the original song not as a goal, but as a starting point. Imitation of great singers is a good first step in your vocal development, but the plan should always be to put your personal spin on every song you perform.

KEY POINTS

Square up your mouth!  Let your larynx rise to a #2 position and constrict your pharynx slightly for an intense, high-frequency sound. Strong abdominal support is required for healthy rock singing.  If you feel a tickle, cough, or need to clear your throat after singing rock, you're doing something wrong.

Use ring, nasality, and brightness as 'cheap volume' rather than constantly using the more dangerous vocal fold volume – which is 'expensive volume.'

For rock, stand tall and brace your entire body for extra support.

# FINAL THOUGHTS

Although it may seem intuitive that the study of singing would encompass many different styles of music, the reality is that most vocal teachers rarely cross styles, so it's up to you to ensure your own success by learning to be proficient in as many as you can. Now more than ever, performers need to be versatile in order to be successful.

Enjoy the process of learning to sing. You will learn much about your body, your emotions, and what's easy or hard for you. We hope that you'll experience the beauty, excitement and gratification that result when you commit yourself fully to vocal and stylistic mastery. You were born with a unique voice and the world can't wait to hear it!

# BONUS TRACK 1
# SOUND EXAMPLES

1.   Straight Tone
2.   Vibrato (wavy tone)
3.   Water Vibrato (straight then wavy tone)
4.   Cry
5.   Creaky Voice
6.   Breathy Voice
7.   Growl
8.   Glides
9.   Fry
10. Yodel
11. Swoops
12. Trill
13. Melisma
14. R&B Run
15. Fry Onset
16. Breathy Onset
17. Soft Glottal Click Onset
18. Stops
19. Neighbor Notes
20. R&B Tails (2-note, 3-note, 5-note)
21. Pop Run
22. Scatting
23. Singers' Syllables (adding syllables)
24. Segmenting Long Phrases
25. Rush and Drag
26. Singing on Resonant Consonants: n, m, ng, v, r, z
27. Fall-Offs
28. Shadow Vowels
29. Air Bursts
30. Vertical Laryngeal Changes
31. Pharynx Widths

Access these clips at <u>singanything.com</u> with the following information:

username:   **singer**
password:   **singnow**

# BONUS TRACK 2
# EXERCISES

## SUPPORT EXERCISE

### Exercise #1: Shh

Sh    sh    sh    sh        shhhhhhhh

## CLASSICAL EXERCISES

### Exercise #2: So

so_____

### Exercise #3: Hung-Oh

hung  oh_____

### Exercise #4: Vah

vah__  vah__  vah__  vah__    vah

### Exercise #5: Eee-Oh

ee__oh__ee_oh___ee__oh__ee__oh__ee__oh__ee_oh___ee__

## MUSICAL THEATER EXERCISES

### Exercise #6:  Bee

bee bee bee bee bee bee bee

### Exercise #7: Ng-Aa

Ng_____aa    aa    aa    aa        aa

### Exercise #8: Yeah-Woh

yeah  yeah  woh woh woh

### Exercise #9:

Can you see the light right aheadof you   showing you the way____

## JAZZ EXERCISES

### Exercise #10:  Moo

moo__ moo__ moo__ moo__  moo

## Exercise #11: I Know

I    know  I know I know I  know

## Exercise #12: Daa Buh Dup Buh Doo Bee

daa___ buh dup__ buh doo__ bee

## Exercise #13: Whenever Night Has Come

Whenever night has come we'll  take  a  ride

## POP EXERCISES

## Exercise #14: Mee-May

mee  may mee  may    mee

## Exercise #15: Naa

naa naa naa naa naa naa naa naa naa naa

## Exercise #16: Come On, Let's Go

Come on let's go__ go__ go_____

## Exercise #17: You Mean Everything To Me

You mean_ ev'rything     ev' ry thing_ to_ me_____

## COUNTRY EXERCISES

## Exercise #18: Hohn

hohn_____

## Exercise #19: Nay

nay  nay  nay  nay   nay nay_   nay

## Exercise #20: Come on Down to a Place I Know

Come  on  down  to  a   place I ____  know_

## Exercise #21: Where Can I Go

Where can I go___ where I'd never stop be-lieve-in at all_____

## R&B EXERCISES

### Exercise #22: Yeah

yeah_____

### Exercise #23: Woh

woh_ woh_ woh_____

### Exercise #24: Loving You Tonight

Lov__ in you_ to night___

### Exercise #25: You're the One for Me

I know that ur the 1 for me_____ yeah_____

## ROCK EXERCISES

### Exercise #26: Yeah

yeah  yeah  yeah  yeah  yeah

### Exercise #27: Naa

naa    naa    naa    naa

### Exercise #28: Get Up and Go

get up and go

### Exercise #29:  Don't Go There

don't__ go__ there____    don't_ go there

You can access the audio clips of all these exercises by logging in at singanything.com with the following information:

username:   singer
password:   singnow

89

# BONUS TRACK 3
# ADDITIONAL EXERCISES

## SUPPORT SYSTEM:

### STEP 1: POSTURE

Imagine yourself being pulled up from the crown of your head like you're a puppet on a string. Now, put one hand up high on your chest and sing a long note. The goal is to keep your chest comfortably lifted for the entire note. If your chest collapses or drops at all, then you need to lift it more.

### STEP 2: BREATHE IN

Try doing the breathing while on 'all fours.' When you breathe in, your belly should drop down toward the floor. When you exhale, your belly should pull in towards your back.

### STEP 3: SING WITH ABDOMINAL SUPPORT

Ribs: Expand your ribs slightly by inhaling. Wrap a stretchy scarf or belt around your expanded ribs. Use the feeling of the scarf or belt to make sure that your ribs are staying out while singing.

Top Belly: Grab a medium size book. Lay down on the ground on your back. Take the book and place it so it lies between your sternum (the bottom of your chest) and your belly button.

Breathe in low and notice that the book goes up. Now, count loudly to 20 firming your top belly out against the book. Now relax and breathe in low again. Then count again and feel the upper belly firm out as you make sound.

**Bottom Belly:** Sitting tall, hum, and gently clutch your bottom belly in. Then open your mouth to breathe and feel your bottom belly relax out. Repeat. Practice this in-and-out motion of your bottom belly. Isolate this movement so no other body part is involved.

## SOUND SYSTEM

## JAW

If your jaw is too tight, it can strain your vocal folds, so we want to make sure your jaw is relaxed. You can check this by putting a pencil across your mouth and holding it loosely behind your 'fang' teeth' on top while letting the pencil rest on your bottom teeth – kinda like a dog holding a bone. Now sing a long 'ah.' If you find yourself biting too hard on the pencil (or if you pull it out and see that you left bite marks), then go back, consciously relax your jaw, and try again.

## TONGUE

Tongue pushups are fun and a great way to get control of your tongue. With the tip of your tongue resting against your bottom teeth, alternately arch and relax the middle of your tongue.

## LARYNX

Having trouble keeping your larynx down? Sing Exercise #2 and try to keep your larynx in the lowered, #4 position. If you feel strainy on the high note, do a plie as you ascend the pitches. This kneebend will help to keep your larynx down and your neck comfortable. Why? Most people reach UP UP UP for high notes. By going DOWN DOWN DOWN, you'll be tricking your larynx into a less-strainy, more-anchored position.

## SOFT PALATE

To gain more control of the lifting of your soft palate, try Exercise #14 by singing "choo" on a long note. Imagine yourself about to sneeze while you're singing it. The almost-sneeze position lifts the soft palate.

## PHARYNX

Find your pharynx access points below your jaw line (see page 21). Widen your pharynx by saying 'Wide' or 'I'm a wide-mouthed frog' (Stylism #31). You'll know you've widened your pharynx when the points POP OUT. This is also known as the 'open throat' feeling. Then with a neutral pharynx, say 'Neutral.' It should sound like a professional radio voice. Then say 'Constricted' and **gently** squeeze only the upper portion of your neck. Never squeeze your larynx or vocal folds.

## RESONANCE

To amplify your <u>ring</u>, put on your ick face, think pointy (by imagining you have a pointy beak, like a bird) and say 'nyee, nyee, nyee'. Listen for the piercingly loud sound that is ring.

To amplify your <u>nasality</u>, drop your face and your soft palate, and say 'maa' several times aiming for a super-buzzy sound.

To amplify your <u>brightness</u>, lift your cheeks and smile, showing 8-10 upper teeth. Say 'I am being very bright' several times. To go darker, cover your upper teeth with your upper lip and say, 'I sound darker.'

## RESONANCE SHAPES

Review your resonator shapes (called Style Shapes) in a mirror by imitating the sketches in each style chapter. That way, when you want to sing a style, you can instantly go to the right shape to help you sound authentic.

| | |
|---|---|
| *Classical:* | *Fish-Face and Inside Smile* |
| *Musical Theater:* | *Molar Mouth* |
| *Jazz:* | *Fish-Lips* |
| *Pop:* | *Smile* |
| *Country:* | *Full Tube (say 'hohn')* |
| *R&B:* | *Water-in-the-Mouth* |
| *Rock:* | *Square Mouth* |

# BONUS TRACK 4
## BASIC VOCAL FOLD FUNCTION

Your vocal folds are folds of muscle covered in mucous membrane whose primary task is to keep food out of our lungs when eating. They also have several other functions:

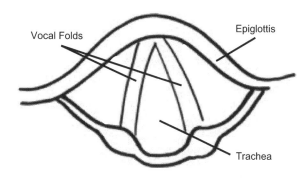

- Valvular: controls lung pressure to aid in lifting weights and defecating.
- Fixative: stabilizes the thorax for efficient arm movement
- Protective: prevents anything other than air from entering the air passages
- Coughing: repels food and dust from entering larynx and clears passage of mucus
- Emotional: creates sounds like crying, laughing, and moaning
- Phonatory: voluntary communication

Your vocal folds fit horizontally in the larynx. They are connected at the front and make a V-shape opening toward the back. These folds open and close VERY fast to create the vocal sound. On the note A below middle C, for example, they open and close 220 times per second. On the note A above middle C, our folds open and close 440 times per second. The high A requires opening and closing at twice that rate: 880 times each second! Amazingly, our brain thinks the pitch, the vocal folds find the correct length, and then they open and close at the correct rate to produce the desired note.

What are the folds made of? A vocal fold at its core is comprised of muscle. This muscle acts as the body of the fold. It's important because as the muscle contracts or relaxes, the length, thickness, and stiffness are all affected. These actions change the vocal sound. Above the body of the vocal fold lies the cover – layers of different kinds of tissue. The uppermost layer is mucous membrane, like in the inside of your mouth. Below this pink and gooey upper layer is a layer similar to rubber bands. The 'rubber bands' become most concentrated at the edge of the vocal fold (the part that touches the other fold when you make sound). This internal edge is called the 'vocal ligament' and is fairly rare in the animal kingdom. Humans, monkeys, and pigs all have a vocal ligament. That's the reason we all can 'squeal' on a high pitch.

Surrounding your folds are all the other parts of your vocal team discussed in this book. For optimal vocal fold health, never squeeze your folds. We all have little pressure sensors called mechanoreceptors in the laryngeal area that allow us to feel if we're squeezing the folds too hard. Your vocal folds are amazing, so be good to them, and they'll reward you with a lifetime of singing!

# DEFINITIONS

**Abdominal muscles:** The muscles on the front and sides of the body between the hips and the ribcage.

**Art Song:** A classical sung piece of serious nature performed with solo singer and piano accompaniment.

**Bel-Canto:** Italian for 'beautiful singing.' A classical style of voice production that began in Flanders in the 14th century and reached its current tenets in Italy early in the 1600s. The features are a lowered larynx, supported air stream, wide and lifted soft palate, tongue position as in the pronunciation of Italian consonants and vowels, legato line, and a relaxed jaw.

**Belting:** Yell-like, and rarely speech-like, singing technique used in such styles as musical theater, R&B, pop, and rock styles. Sounds like 'chest voice' on higher notes.

**Classical Vocal Technique:** For women, the predominant use of a heady sound, though men sing with deep, covered sound. This technique includes a lowered larynx, wide pharynx, and raised soft palate. Used in opera, operetta, choir singing, and (modified) in 'legit' musical theater.

**Contemporary Commercial Music (CCM):** Replaces the older term 'non-classical.' It includes the vocal styles pop, jazz, R&B, gospel, rock, country, folk, and sometimes musical theater belting.

**Diaphragm:** The large, dome-shaped muscle that sits below your lungs and controls breathing. When the diaphragm contracts downward, the lungs are pulled open for inhalation.

**Diaphragmatic (or Abdominal) Breathing:** The manner of breathing most beneficial for singers in which the chest and ribcage remain expanded, but still while the abdomen relaxes out for air intake.

**Dynamics:** Musical markings that suggest softer or louder singing.

**Hard Palate:** The hard part of the roof the mouth behind the front teeth.

**Jazz:** The style created originally by African-Americans in the early 1900s. Distinctive characteristics are the use of improvisation, bent pitches or 'blues' notes (flat 3, 5, and 7), swing, and polyrhythms.

**Larynx:** The voice box. A complex set of cartilages, muscles, and membranes that sit on top of the windpipe. It moves up and down when swallowing. The vocal folds (also known as vocal cords) lay horizontally, front to back, within the larynx.

**Lean:** When trying to maintain a 'talky' sound as the pitch ascends, lean (short for 'laryngeal lean') is felt by the singer as the forward pull of the hyoid bone.

**Legit:** The musical theater vocal style with classical influences. From the word 'legitimate.'

**Lungs:** The two large, spongy sacs within the chest cavity used for breathing.

**Musical Theater:** A form of theater that combines songs, dialogue, acting, and dance. Also known as 'musicals.'

**Nasality:** Resonance resulting from vocal fold sound passing by a lowered soft palate and entering the nose.

**Notes:** A musical pitch that is sung or played, spelled with the letters A-G.

**Opera:** A dramatic musical work, in the classical style, which combines singers, orchestra, chorus, sets, and costumes. Originated at the end of the 1500s.

**Operetta:** A lighter, less dramatic version of opera. Often, it is of a comic nature (such as in the work of Gilbert & Sullivan) or sentimental (as in the works of Franz Lehar and Sigmund Romberg).

**Oratorio:** A musical setting with orchestra, chorus, and soloists of sacred texts. Operatic in style but without scenery, costumes, or action.

**Pharynx:** The throat space above the larynx and behind the mouth and nose. An important resonating chamber.

**Pop Style:** A music and vocal style intended for commercial success. Highly produced, packaged, and marketed.

**R&B (Rhythm and Blues):** A group of African-American vocal styles including soul, blues, spirituals, gospel, and hip-hop.

**Resonance:** The filtering of harmonics within the vocal tract that creates vocal timbre.

**Resonance Feel:** The sensation of vibrations felt by the singer while singing.

**Rhythms:** How long or short notes are to be held.

**Ribs:** The long, curved bones that form the ribcage surrounding the chest.

**Ring:** The piercing or metallic resonance that 'carries' the voice. Creates the illusion of greater power.

**Rock Style:** Originating in the late 1950s as 'rock & roll,' this style tends to be a loud pop style with strong, rhythmic beats and amplified, electric instruments.

**Sternum:** Also known as the 'breastbone,' the sternum is located in the middle of the chest and connects the ribs.

**Support:** Short for 'abdominal breath support,' this muscular action of the lower belly pulling inwards against the upper belly firming outwards creates much of the air pressure needed to vibrate the vocal folds.

**Syncopation:** Rhythm that emphasizes the weak beats. Used frequently in jazz.

**Tempo:** The speed of the beat in music.

**Tone:** The quality or character of a sound – for example, dark and heavy versus light and airy.

**Torso:** Also called the trunk, the main portion of the body including the chest and abdomen. Limbs and neck are attached to the torso.

**Vibrato:** A regular, pulsating change of pitch. Used in singing and instrumental playing as an ornament to enhance expressivity.

**Vocal Folds or Vocal Cords:** Two bands of muscle with mucosal covering, inside the larynx, which vibrate together to create sound.

Made in the USA
San Bernardino, CA
28 October 2013